Gertrude
Stein
Remembered

Gertrude Stein Remembered

LINDA SIMON

University of Nebraska Press, Lincoln and London

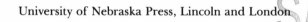

Acknowledgments
for material in collections and
for previously published material appear
on the first page of chapter texts and constitute an extension of the copyright page.
© 1994 by the University of Nebraska Press. All
rights reserved. Manufactured in the United States
of America. ⊗ The paper in this book meets the mini-
mum requirements of American National Standard
for Information Sciences – Permanence of Paper for
Printed Library Materials, ANSI Z39.48-1984. Library
of Congress Cataloging in Publication Data. Simon,
Linda, 1946–   Gertrude Stein remembered / Linda
Simon. p. cm. Includes bibliographical references (p.)
and index. ISBN 0-8032-4240-9 1. Stein, Gertrude,
1874–1946 – Biography. 2. Women authors,
American – 20th century – Biography.
3. Americans – France – Paris – Biography.
I. Title. PS3537.T323Z8235   1994
818'.5209 dc20 [B]
94-4246 CIP

CONTENTS

CONTENTS

PLATES

INTRODUCTION

I read a poem of George Eliot when I was very young
I can not often remember poetry but I can remember
that. May I join the choir invisible of those immortal
dead who live again.

Everybody's Autobiography

I

Gertrude Stein surely has joined the choir of immortals whose work
speaks to generation after generation of readers. Those readers have
formed their own image of Stein based on her two volumes of autobiography, *The Autobiography of Alice B. Toklas* and *Everybody's Autobiography,* her essays, and the many volumes of her experiments in poetry
and prose. From these texts, Gertrude Stein has emerged as a complex, sometimes contradictory, woman. Some see her as the mother of
us all, a feisty feminist who railed against the linearity and patriarchal
connotations of the English language. Others see her as a lesbian who
spent her early years oppressed by a society into which she did not fit,
finally achieving a measure of personal liberation in Paris. Because of
her literary experiments, some align her with Samuel Beckett, James
Joyce, and Ezra Pound and portray her as a lone eccentric. Because of
her association with the art world of Paris, others place her alongside

Pablo Picasso and Georges Braque and see her as a Bohemian, blithely flaunting convention.

Gertrude Stein was all of these, a multiplicity of moods and energies. We encounter her in her own texts, and we discover her again in the vivid memories of her friends, neighbors, rivals, and colleagues. This collection gathers twenty-one memoirs of men and women who knew Stein from her undergraduate days at Radcliffe College until her death in 1946. Some adored her; some disdained her; some felt close to her; some believed that she would allow no one to get close enough. Stein herself believed that her identity as an artist differed essentially from her social or public personality. 'The thing one gradually comes to find out,' she wrote in 'What Are Masterpieces and Why Are There So Few of Them,' 'is that one has no identity that is when one is in the act of doing anything. Identity is recognition, you know who you are because you and others remember anything about yourself but essentially you are not that when you are doing anything. I am I because my little dog knows me but, creatively speaking the little dog knowing that you are you and your recognising that he knows, that is what destroys creation.'[1]

Identity was an important concern of Stein's, perhaps the most important, and a concern that she shared with many of her contemporaries. Like her mentor William James, she wondered about the inner selves that lie hidden beneath one's public personality. Like many of her fellow writers – F. Scott Fitzgerald, for example, and Guillaume Apollinaire – she celebrated the idea of breaking with one's past to create a new personality in a new context. '[T]he ones who had survived had made some sort of clean break,' Fitzgerald wrote in *The Crack Up*. 'A clean break is something you cannot come back from; that is irretrievable because it makes the past cease to exist.'[2] Like Picasso and Ernest Hemingway, she exuberantly honed a public image and advertised that image in her popular works. But for Stein, a writer's true identity needed to be protected from intrusion, even by readers.

Introduction

'I am coming to see that power real power comes from the part of withdrawal, that necessitates choosing an image. My image is in my wording.'[3]

> But I had a family. They can be a nuisance in identity
> but there is no doubt no shadow of doubt that that
> identity the family identity we can do without.
>
> *Geographical History of America*

Gertrude Stein was born on February 3, 1874, in Allegheny, Pennsylvania, the daughter of Daniel Stein and Amelia (Keyser) Stein. A businessman, her father – like a German Jewish Clarence Day – was authoritarian and given to bursts of irrational anger. Because her mother usually acquiesced to his wishes, their five children were convinced that she was passive and ineffectual. The youngest of the family, Stein grew up feeling 'the most cut off'[4] from her parents and siblings. Only Leo, the brother closest in age, shared some of her interests and sensibilities.

After the family spent a few years traveling in Europe when Gertrude was very young, they settled in Oakland, California, the city that earned Stein's famous remark: 'There is no there there.'[5] Her imagination was stirred by the books she read voraciously. Shakespeare, Trollope, Richardson, Defoe all took her far from the mundane middle-class world of Oakland, and the oppression of her family life. She portrayed herself as a solitary child who took 'every possible excuse to be alone so that I might dream, might lose myself in intense emotions by the side of which all else paled into insignificance.'[6]

Her feelings of isolation and alienation crystallized in adolescence. She called this period the 'dark and dreadful days' when she felt fearful and anxious. She did not fit into the conventional Victorian ideal of femininity, nor did she want to. She knew what was expected of her:

to marry, to be 'willing to take everything and be satisfied to live in Belmont in a large house with a view and plenty of flowers and neighbors who were cousins and some friends who did not say anything.'[7] She hoped that a college education would give her some measure of independence from these expectations, and also would allow her the opportunity of 'finding out what was inside myself to make me what I was.'[8] In 1893, she followed Leo to Cambridge, Massachusetts and enrolled in the Harvard Annex, precursor to Radcliffe College. There, she studied with William James, George Santayana, Josiah Royce, and Hugo Munsterberg, among others. Because Stein was interested in pursuing studies in psychology, James suggested that she take a medical degree. In 1897, she entered the Johns Hopkins Medical School. Leo, too, was in Baltimore studying biology.

The years at Johns Hopkins were difficult both personally and academically. She was forced to confront her lesbianism when she fell in love with a fellow student, who spurned her. And she realized that she did not like medical school, particularly courses in obstetrics and gynecology. In the spring of 1901, Stein fell to her lowest point academically, failing four courses. It was her last semester at Johns Hopkins. Again, she fled by following her brother Leo, who had gone to Europe – first London, and later Paris. By 1903, she had settled with him at 27, rue de Fleurus.

III

[T]hey surround you with a civilised atmosphere and they leave you inside of you completely to yourself.

Paris, France

Many writers and artists – American and European – emigrated to Paris early in the century, seeking an environment in which to create works that were not understood or encouraged in their native lands. More importantly, they wanted to recreate themselves, to free themselves from a claustrophobic past and stultifying present. Stein once commented that Americans could not become artists at home, only dentists. Her sentiments were echoed by her fellow expatriates.

Those who knew Stein in Paris from 1903 to 1906 describe a quiet, self-effacing woman who seemed dominated by her voluble older brother, a self-described expert on aesthetics. Stein had just begun, tentatively, to refer to herself as a writer, but she had little confidence in her ability. Her current projects were *Three Lives, The Making of Americans,* and *Things As They Are.* In each of these works, Stein set herself the problem of portraying the 'bottom nature' of her characters. Although *Three Lives* was influenced by Gustave Flaubert's *Trois Contes,* all of the works drew upon Stein's own life, especially her experiences in Baltimore.

Stein's brother Michael and his wife, Sarah, had also settled in Paris. Through these relatives, Stein was drawn into a lively world of artists and writers. But she was hardly central to that world. Her life changed, however, when Alice Toklas came to visit, fell in love with Gertrude, and ended up staying as her companion. When Toklas supplanted Leo in Stein's household, Stein supplanted him in the salon on the rue de Fleurus. From the testimony of Daniel-Henri Kahnweiler, Natalie Clifford Barney, and Sylvia Beach, we can see that Stein became more out-going, 'magnetic,' as Barney described her, and increasingly confident, with no reticence about expressing her many opinions on art and literature.

Stein's reputation as a cultural figure comes largely from her brilliant circle of friends. Her home was a meeting place for many accomplished and aspiring artists, such as Pavel Tchelitchew, Man Ray, Jacques Lipchitz, the photographers Alvin Langdon Coburn, Cecil Beaton, and Carl Van Vechten, and, of course, Henri Matisse and Picasso. Some of these artists recall Stein in memoirs reprinted here.

Writers tended to have a more volatile relationship with Stein. Her friendship with Hemingway dissolved into bitterness; she lost her esteem for Fitzgerald. But she maintained admiration for Sherwood Anderson and Thornton Wilder, who championed her work and professed enthusiasm for her literary experiments.

The memoirs included in this volume testify to the different kinds of relationships she had with writers at different stages of her life, from the 1920s, when she was aspiring for recognition, to the 1930s and '40s, when she was considered a literary lion by the young men and women who came to pay homage to her. She could be charming and warm, as Sylvia Beach remembers, describing a meeting between Stein and Sherwood Anderson; she could be 'biblical' and 'monumental,' as Robert McAlmon portrays her.

By the time Stein returned to America in 1934, after the critical success of *The Autobiography of Alice B. Toklas,* she was a legend in her own time. People who flocked to meet her expected to see an odd, heavy-set woman wearing sandals, long skirts, and unlikely vests, accompanied by her stern, homely 'secretary.' They expected her to ramble unintelligibly about texts that they found nonsensical. They expected her to be pretentious and condescending. Many discovered, instead, a warm, ebullient woman who looked more like a beloved grandmother than a literary anarchist. Her lectures were not only clear and direct, but funny. She had an easy smile and a genuine interest in other people. She was happy to share her ideas, happy to be back in the United States – happy to be creating modern literature. Many of her admirers attest to this image of Gertrude Stein, and they were right: she was a gregarious woman who enjoyed popular acclaim. She cared for younger writers, cherished her friends, lavished food, attention, and kindness on her visitors.

Gertrude Stein Remembered includes selections by men and women – among them novelists, journalists, and artists – whose lives touched Stein's. They rescue Stein from the choir invisible of our literary past and revive a woman who once wrote, with hope and conviction:

Introduction

I shall not speak for anybody. I shall do my duty, I shall establish that mile. I shall choose wonder. Be blest.[9]

NOTES

1. Patricia Meyrowitz, ed., *Gertrude Stein: Writings and Lectures 1909–1945* (Baltimore: Penguin, 1971), pp.148–49.
2. F. Scott Fitzgerald, 'Pasting It Together,' in *The Crack Up,* ed. Edmund Wilson (New York: New Directions, 1956), p.81.
3. Gertrude Stein, *As Fine As Melanctha* (New Haven: Yale University Press, 1954), p.167.
4. Gertrude Stein, *Making of Americans* (New York: Something Else Press, 1966), p.416.
5. Gertrude Stein, *Everybody's Autobiography* (New York: Vintage, 1973 [1937]), p.289.
6. Rosalind S. Miller, 'In the Red Deeps,' *Gertrude Stein: Form and Intelligibility* (New York: Exposition Press, 1949).
7. Gertrude Stein, 'If You Had Three Husbands,' *Geography and Plays* (Boston: Four Seas, 1922).
8. Gertrude Stein, 'The Gradual Making of the Making of Americans,' in *Selected Writings of Gertrude Stein,* ed. Carl Van Vechten (New York: Vintage, 1962), p.212.
9. Gertrude Stein, 'Pink Melon Joy,' *Geography and Plays,* pp.374–75.

Gertrude
Stein
Remembered

Alvin Langdon Coburn. *Portrait of Gertrude Stein* (1913). Courtesy, International Museum of Photography, George Eastman House, Rochester.

ARTHUR LACHMAN

Arthur Lachman's memoir, along with the unsigned obituary that follows, are among the few documents that survive pertaining to Gertrude Stein's years at Radcliffe. She entered the college – then called the Harvard Annex – in 1893, joining her brother Leo in Cambridge, and left in 1898, when she enrolled in medical school at Johns Hopkins on the advice of her favorite professor, William James.

In 'Gertrude Stein as I Knew Her,' Lachman is mistaken on two counts – Stein's age when he knew her (she was a bit younger than 24) – and her hair, which she did not wear short until many years later. But he does characterize well the atmosphere of Hugo Munsterberg's psychology laboratory and Stein's work with Leon Solomons. Both Stein and Solomons were students of William James, one of the strongest influences from Stein's early years. Stein was an enthusiastic, if erratic, student, but Solomons, according to James, was a genius. 'Certainly the *keenest* intellect we ever had,' he wrote to Munsterberg after Solomons's death, 'and one of the loftiest characters! But there was always a mysterious side to me about his mind: he appeared so critical and destructive, and yet kept alluding all the while to ethical and religious ideals of his own which he wished to live for, and of which he never vouchsafed a glimpse to anyone else. He was the only student I have ever had of whose criticism I felt afraid: and that was partly because

I never quite understood the region from which they came, and with the authority of which he spoke.'[1]

'Normal Motor Automatism,' published in the *Psychological Review*, September 1896, and 'Cultivated Motor Automatism: A Study of Character in its Relation to Attention,' appearing in the same journal in May, 1898, were Stein's first publications. Lachman reminds us that spiritualism was an important inspiration for this research, but we need to understand spiritualism not only as a belief in ghosts and non-corporeal consciousness, but also as a means to understand layers of consciousness.

In the years before Freud, with no schema to map human consciousness, psychologists and philosophers sought a means to bring an individual's hidden inner selves to the surface. Automatic writing was one means to that end. Although Stein insisted that the experiments did not prove successful when she sat as a subject, she, like many of her contemporaries, was interested in exploring what she called the 'bottom nature' of friends and acquaintances.

Photographs of Stein from the late 1890s show a pretty young woman, plump to be sure, with an open smile and intelligent eyes. Both Lachman and Stein's classmates at Radcliffe note the genuine warmth and interest in other people that characterized Stein throughout her life.

1. Henry James, III, ed., *Letters of William James*, vol.2. (Boston: Atlantic Monthly Press, 1920), p.119.

Gertrude Stein
as I Knew Her

Gertrude Stein's influence on American literature for nearly fifty years has been tremendous. Whether for weal or for woe will be debated for perhaps fifty years more. The purpose of these notes is not to evaluate her work but is rather an attempt to understand the evolution of a complex character which impressed itself upon the world at large over a long period of time.

In many ways the development of the human mind may be compared to the physical development of insect life. There is a larval stage which can be observed and there finally emerges a full-blown moth, butterfly, or cockroach with an intermediate chrysalis stage which completely escapes observation. This is probably true of all personalities who greatly impress themselves upon their contemporaries after a more or less obscure beginning. All of us can think of examples of this sudden emergence of a forceful personality into the world of observation.

I knew Gertrude Stein during her chrysalis stage when we both belonged to a small group of earnest young people at Harvard University. At this time she was about twenty-four years old. She was a heavy-set, ungainly young woman, very mannish in her appearance. Her hair was cut short at a time when this was by no means the fashion among

From the Gertrude Stein Collection, Yale Collection of American Literature, Beinecke Rare Book and Manuscript Library, Yale University. Published by permission of the Yale University Library.

the fair sex. She always wore black, and her somewhat ample figure was never corseted. She was, in fact, frequently untidy in appearance and her garments were not always neat.

We met every Saturday afternoon, and most of Sunday, at the home of a hospitable mother whose son and daughter were in college; and I have little doubt that at times she felt the strain of hearty appetites and of even more vigorous arguments and discussions. One of our chief stimuli came from regular attendance every Sunday at the lectures held at Harvard Chapel. These were given by a succession of clergymen of various faiths; and they were more in the nature of enlightenment on the subject of comparative religion, than narrowly parochial. Very few of the visiting preachers forgot themselves and launched into invective. Our Sunday night review of what we had listened to lasted too often far into Monday's wee small hours.

Gertrude gave no indication during this period that she was later to make her place in the artistic and literary world of Paris. She was rather awkward with her hands. She could not draw; she did none of the needlework or knitting that is woman's outlet for excess energy; and she played no musical instrument.

Moreover, Gertrude Stein was never a real student. Although she states in her autobiography, which she thinly veiled as *The Autobiography of Alice B. Toklas,* her secretary, that for two years she did quite brilliant work in the medical school at Johns Hopkins, an old friend of mine who knew her then and who later became a Nobel-prize winner in medicine has told me that she was a very indifferent pupil. In any event, she failed to graduate.

As for her knowledge of chemistry, which is my own field, I recall one time she tried to give me a lesson. We were making some taffy for candy pulling, and I was melting butter in some tin pie plates. Said Gertrude, 'Don't you know better than that? When you melt butter it forms butyric acid. Butyric acid dissolves tin and tin is poisonous.' When I pointed out that all three of these assertions were erroneous, she answered in the words of the old Italian epigram, '*Si non e vero e bene trovato.*'

Her activities when I knew her, and probably throughout her life, may best be summed up in a quotation from Montaigne: 'The most fruitful and natural exercise of the mind, in my opinion, is conversation; I find the use of it more sweet than that of any other activity of life.'

To this art of conversation she brought an intelligence that even at this early stage of her career was remarkably keen and an obvious gift for fascinating a great variety of people. Although even then she had no 'passion for anonymity,' she did not show the almost morbid craving for adulation that was perhaps the key to her later development.

During this formative period of her career, Gertrude Stein took part in some experiments which were to have a profound influence on her later work. This was a study of automatic writing initiated in the winter of 1895 and spring of 1896 by Leon M. Solomons and myself. After I left Harvard, Gertrude Stein became my successor in this collaboration.

In an article entitled 'Has Gertrude Stein a Secret?' Professor B. F. Skinner (*Atlantic Monthly*, January 1934) some years ago discussed these experiments, but the account there given of the origin of the repetitive phrase 'A rose is a rose is a rose' is not entirely correct. Professor Skinner could have had no personal information or knowledge of this work for the simple reason that it was done before he was born. I know that his account is inaccurate because, to paraphrase some historical writer, 'Much of this I saw and some of it I was.'

Before outlining the experimental work just mentioned, which in itself proved to be of little eventual importance, it is necessary to give an account of the personality of Leon Mendez Solomons, who conducted it. Solomons, who died an untimely death at the age of twenty-seven, was one of the most remarkable men it has been my good fortune to know, and it has been my privilege to know a great many outstanding men in various fields of knowledge. He was a man of unusual mental powers and strongly impressed his ability on all who were fortunate enough to know him, even to more or less casual acquaintances. While not a dominating personality, he was widely read, deeply thoughtful, and enormously stimulating.

From the time I first knew him in high school, Solomons and I were practically inseparable. We both took the course in chemistry at the University of California and thereafter he went on to Cambridge, specializing first in mathematical physics and later switching to psychology. When I joined him there somewhat later, the experiments referred to by Skinner were initiated.

We all have our quirks and soft spots, and when I first knew him, Solomons' soft spot was spiritualism. This interest, or one might say obsession, he had acquired from his family, who were devout believers in occult phenomena. Gradually, as his acquaintance with physical science grew, and perhaps due partly to my own rather practical point of view, this interest in the occult ceased to be personal on his part and became detached. Together we had read studies on this subject by eminent scientists such as Crooks, Lodge, James, Zollner, and others.

At Cambridge this subject came up again for discussion between us, influenced perhaps by the studies that had then been made by Professor William James. The eminent scientists named had all devoted themselves primarily to making sure that trickery in spiritualistic manifestations had been eliminated. This, of course, was a somewhat unscientific attitude for eminent scientists to take. It amounted to saying 'If I cannot prove it is wrong, it must be right.' It is simply a manifestation of the only too common point of view that if you are not for me you are against me.

In considering our experimental approach, Leon and I came to the conclusion that the only one open to us in which trickery was definitely ruled out lay in the study of automatic phenomena, or more particularly, what is known as automatic writing. Our experimental

6

method was quite simple. One of us would be armed with pencil or Ouija board, and the other would read aloud to him. The pencil was allowed to work its will and at the end of the experiment the 'readee' attempted to recall what had been read to him. At times we even went so far that the subject would be reading one story and manipulating the pencil at the same time, whereas the other operator would read an entirely different story.

It may be said here that on the whole these experiments were inconclusive. They proved that this phenomenon was merely one aspect of a rather common ability of the human mind. Any good court reporter is an example of how the finger can perform accurately while the mind is partly distracted elsewhere. A still more striking example is the ability of many accomplished pianists to perform intricate sonatas while at the same time carrying on a lively conversation.

At the start of the experiments, the markings on the paper consisted almost exclusively of doodlings. Later, words appeared, frequently misspelled. Once in a while, but infrequently, sentences would appear, their subject matter quite irrelevant. Solomons became more proficient at the writing of words than I did, and judging from Gertrude Stein's account, she herself was none too successful in getting much beyond the doodling stage.

The experiments were discontinued shortly after Gertrude Stein took over and were briefly published by her in the *Harvard Psychological Review,* constituting the first writing of hers ever to be printed.

Though the experiments in themselves proved of little importance, their chief characteristic was that repetition of isolated and more or less meaningless words upon which Gertrude herself later rose to fame. This was the real origin of 'this is a rose is a rose is a rose.' Though in her autobiography Stein makes but brief and anonymous reference to Solomons as 'a young philosopher and mathematician who was doing research work in psychology and who left a definite mark on her life,' it is unlikely that she could or did escape the impact of such a mind as Solomons's upon her own. Whether unconsciously or deliberately, her literary style undoubtedly stems from her experiments in automatic writing.

Another person who had a great influence on the development of G.S. was her brother Leo, with whom she lived in Paris after her unsuccessful attempt to graduate in medicine. He lived in Cambridge at the time I speak of, but we saw little of him. He was reserved, neurotic, probably partly ill, and his chief interest lay in the field of art. It was he who aroused in her, during their residence together in Paris, that interest in art or at least artists which became one of her passions.

However, Leo subjected his sister to constant criticism and was not impressed by her later development. His characterization of her in his posthumous work, *Journey into the Self,* does not lack frankness: 'Gertrude . . . hungers and thirsts after *gloire,* and it was of course a serious thing for her that I can't abide her stuff and think it abominable. . . . Both Picasso and Gertrude are using their intellects, which they ain't got, to do what would need the finest critical tact, which they ain't got neither, and are turning out the most Godalmighty rubbish that is to be found. . . . If Gertrude had been able to express herself effectively in English she would never have taken to jargon. . . . Anyone so stupid as that can hardly have a dependable sensitiveness. . . . I simply cannot take Gertrude seriously as a literary phenomenon.' Small wonder that they often quarreled and finally separated.

On reading through Gertrude Stein's autobiography, one is struck by two features which were not present in the girl of over fifty years ago. One is her inordinate vanity. In her autobiography she calls herself, and I quote: 'one of the three geniuses she has known,' the others being Picasso and Professor Whitehead. Perhaps an author's vanity is a necessary factor in his productivity.

The other development which cannot fail to strike the reader of this book is her almost morbid craving for recognition. It annoyed her that for many years she was not listed in *Who's Who in America,* which is

8

a cheap form of fame for one whose autobiography reads like a roster of every artistic or literary personage who ever came to Paris. Perhaps she wanted to show her annoying brother Leo just 'who is who in our family.'

Said the Autocrat of the Breakfast Table: 'Never mind what your cousins, brothers, sisters, aunts and uncles and the rest say about that fine work you have written. Send it to the editors.'

Neither of these traits was present in the Gertrude Stein I knew and admired. Moreover, she was far too intelligent to have gone in for the mummery she practiced in Paris for so many years. The picture of her in a Grecian gown, sitting in the center of her large Paris salon and receiving the homage and adulation of a large crowd, just does not jibe with the young woman I used to know in Cambridge fifty years ago.

These notes are purely in a reminiscent vein, and no attempt will be made here to evaluate Gertrude Stein's personal contribution to contemporary literature. Professor Skinner's analysis of her writings will be found illuminating with reference to their underlying psychology.

Skinner's feeling seems to be that Gertrude Stein had a second personality, but that the second one was of a very flimsy nature. This second part has the characteristics of automatic writing. Skinner declines to estimate the literary value of a good deal of Stein's writing. He suggests that part of it is pretty good, but that the rest of it might well be forgotten. I imagine that most of us have very much the same feeling about her.

In Memoriam

Gertrude Stein, 1898

In the death of Gertrude Stein in Neuilly, France, on July 27, 1946, Radcliffe has lost one of its noted graduates, a legend in the world of literature and art, famous throughout the world. Because there are few facts of her two score years in France which have escaped public print and because her prodigious literary output is so well known to readers in her native America as elsewhere, the *Quarterly*, in the tribute which follows, does not attempt to present a well-rounded life history of Radcliffe's distinguished Alumna. Rather, we seek to convey, through intimate anecdotes, the impression that Gertrude Stein made on her Radcliffe friends of the 1890's, three of whom have graciously allowed us to draw this composite picture from material they submitted at the request of the Secretary of 1898, Florence Locke Lawrence. – *The Editor*

Gertrude Stein seems to have been known by very few undergraduates of her time. She lived in a private student house with seven or eight others and was part of a small circle of brilliant men and women students who met in a Cambridge home. What set her apart from all the others was her personal quality. Knowing her intimately enhanced every interest one had. To attend a symphony concert or an opera with

First published in the *Radcliffe Quarterly* (August 1946: 21). © Radcliffe College, 1946. Reprinted with permission of the Radcliffe Quarterly.

My thanks to Carol Kountz for bringing to my attention this obituary. *Ed.*

her was to gain new enjoyment from it. To live in that small student house with her was to feel that rare, warm, human quality which not only brought famous people to see her in Paris but made the G.I.'s flock to her home when she was past seventy.

She came to Radcliffe in 1893, at the age of nineteen, to be near her brother Leo, who was studying at Harvard, and to share in the sort of education he was getting. Their parents were dead, and Gertrude and Leo, the two youngest of five children, had always been very good companions. Gertrude was admitted to Radcliffe as a special student on the strength of a letter that she wrote to the Academic Board, setting forth her reasons for wanting to study there. Her formal education had been desultory, given largely by tutors and interrupted by family sojourns in Europe. She had read enormously, and she brought with her a library of English classics, poetry, and history which filled from floor to ceiling the wall of a large room. (When she was eleven or twelve, her family thought they were headed for a financial crash, and so Gertrude and Leo had taken all the money they had and bought books as the best insurance against a dreary future. The family weathered the crisis, and they had the books anyway, and lived in them.)

As a special student, Gertrude Stein seems to have been admitted almost at once to courses designed for graduate students, and much of her work was done in small groups in laboratories at Harvard. History, philosophy, and psychology were her major interests, especially experimental psychology as it was beginning under Professor Münsterberg. She did work in association, which some think may perhaps have been the starting point for her peculiar literary style. Later she was probably also influenced by the philosophy of Henri Bergson.

William James was a great friend of hers, and it was by his advice that she decided to take the course in medicine at Johns Hopkins, as a preparation for further study of psychology. This raised the question of a B.A. degree from Radcliffe as a prerequisite and the passing of those overlooked entrance examinations. It took fifteen exams to enter Radcliffe in those days, and by 1897, when Gertrude Stein had finished her college work for a degree *magna cum laude,* she still had an entrance test in advanced Latin to take.

In her approach to the problem of learning Latin may be found one of the keys to her life. She was always doing what was most significant for her at the time. To know Latin was not significant for her, but she had to pass Latin to do what was significant – study at Johns Hopkins. She put off the real study of Latin until the last moment, carrying a Latin grammar under her arm and apparently hoping she might absorb it through her pores. One of her anxious friends taught her that *isieme esiumibus* were the endings of the third declension, but it is doubtful that she knew where the dividing lines came. She wrote a *Caesar* examination that she said was very consistent, either all right or all wrong. Then in fun she used the Bible as oracle to see if she had passed, and found her finger on a passage in *Lamentations.* The prophecy was true. *E* would have meant failure, but her mark was *F.* She spent her summer gaily in Europe and the next year learned and passed Latin.

She was awarded her degree from Radcliffe with the Class of 1898, after she had already completed one year of brilliant work at Johns Hopkins. Graduation from Johns Hopkins was not significant for her, but it was significant to protest a course in obstetrics which she thought should not be required. So she refused to take the course and got no degree.

She was absolutely indifferent to conventions. On one occasion, for instance, when she could think of no proper ending for a theme and was impatient to close, she simply wrote, 'Well, good-by, gentlemen.'

She enjoyed being different, and once remarked that what she wished for was more *gloire* – a wish that seems to have been fulfilled in her later years. Just as she refused to be bound by conventionalities, she refused also to be bound by loyalties to her past associations.

She was wholly unconcerned as to what people might think of her unconventionality and refused to be governed by what they thought she should do. Already in her college days she refused to be bound by the dictates of style, though she then dressed on the whole conventionally. She clung to one particular 'sailor hat' until it became so disreputable that a friend placed it deep in an ash barrel.

An active member of the Radcliffe philosophy club, she loved discussion and not infrequently was as willing to talk on one side of a subject as the other. She was sometimes rather overpowering in argument and so asserted her opinions as to leave her opponent feeling somewhat futile and flattened out, though usually of the same opinion still. Her well-developed sense of humor, her originality, her clear, active mind, quick in association, made her a brilliant conversationalist.

When her Radcliffe friends think of Gertrude Stein, it is of a good companion with a genuine warmth of interest in those about her. She knew how to enjoy life and could lead others to enjoy it with her. She has always been like a magnet to young people who loved intellectual freedom, and it is easy to understand why young writers, artists, and American G.I.'s were attracted to her.

L.W.S., '98; M.L.E., '96; L.S.E., '90

DANIEL-HENRI KAHNWEILER

Daniel-Henri Kahnweiler, born in Germany in 1884, emigrated to Paris in his early twenties, disappointing his parents by not pursuing a profession. By the time he was twenty-three, he had opened a small art gallery at 28, rue Vignon, near the Madeleine, featuring the works of the most daring young artists in Paris. Kahnweiler enthusiastically launched the careers of 'the lucid Frenchman Braque and the fanatically searching Spaniard Picasso,' Juan Gris, and André Derain.

In 1908, Kahnweiler mounted a formal exhibition to introduce Georges Braque to the Parisian art world. But he soon discovered that he need not go to such efforts. Without spending any money on publicity, without submitting his artists' works to the salons, he found that he had a bustling business.

Kahnweiler became a champion of the cubists, largely because he inspired faith among both the artists and his customers. He refused to consider the artists as proponents of any school, but rather as individuals working out their own language of art. The artists known as 'cubists,' he wrote in *The Rise of Cubism*, 'cared very little whether they were called that or something else.' Instead, he tried to understand the 'inner urge' of painters grappling with the enduring artistic 'tasks of painting: to represent three dimensions and color on a flat surface, and to comprehend them in the unity of that surface.'

Kahnweiler served to defend, explain, and promote modern art to collectors with a range of interests and understanding. Among those

Man Ray, *Alice B. Toklas and Gertrude Stein, Rue de Fleurus, Paris 1922*. The Baltimore Museum of Art: Cone Archives, Bequest of Etta Cone, 1950. BMA 1950.85.5.

15

collectors were the Steins: Sarah and her husband, Michael; Gertrude and her brother, Leo. He met them, he tells us in this memoir, when they were negotiating to buy a painting from Matisse. A warm friendship began, but it was interrupted by World War I, when Kahnweiler, a German citizen, was forced to flee from Paris. When he returned in 1920, he and his wife were frequent guests at 27, rue de Fleurus, where Gertrude then lived with Alice Toklas.

Unlike some of Stein's more literary friends, Kahnweiler was sympathetic to Stein's experiments in prose. During the war, when she and Toklas were in Mallorca, Stein had written a spate of poems, portraits, and sketches, largely unintelligible to most readers. But Kahnweiler believed that Stein's experiments echoed the work that his artists were doing, and he suggested that he publish her work. Not surprisingly, this gesture endeared Kahnweiler to Stein.

Introduction to
Painted Lace

How did I meet Gertrude Stein? When Carl Van Vechten asked me to
write the introduction to this fifth volume of her posthumous work, I
began to consider what I had to say about her and first of all attempted
to recall how we had met. At first it seemed to me that there could be
no question – of course I had met her at Picasso's, in the atelier on
the Rue Ravignan. But, thinking about it, I was surprised to discover
that it was through Matisse that I began my association with her. This
happened indirectly.

In April 1907 I was preparing to open the small gallery that I had
just rented at 28 Rue Vignon, not far from the Madeleine. I had got in
touch with the painters whose work I had been noticing over the past
several years in the Salon des Indépendants and the Salon d'Automne.
The Salon des Indépendants, which was then held in the conservato-
ries in the Cours-La-Reine, had just opened – in the month of March
to be exact. I had again come upon canvases by these painters and had
acquired several of them. The journalist Louis Vauxcelles had some
time before termed these artists the 'Fauves,' and history has retained
this name for them. I knew Derain, Vlaminck, and Braque. I also knew
Matisse, whose pictures that year dominated the room devoted to the
Fauves, and went often to see him in his apartment-atelier on the Quai

From *Painted Lace* by Gertrude Stein (New Haven: Yale University Press, 1955), introduction by Daniel-Henri Kahnweiler. © 1955 by Yale University Press, reprinted by
permission.

Saint Michel. His conversation, filled with perception, subtlety, and wit, interested me deeply. It was too late for me to become his dealer, for he was already signed up with the Bernheims. Nevertheless, he asked me one day if I would undertake the following business transaction: Two collectors whom he knew, a Mr. and Mrs. Stein, wanted to acquire a picture of his called *La Coiffeuse*. He showed me the painting, which I thought very handsome. Now, he explained, these people are not paying the whole amount necessary for the sale, but they own a small head by Gauguin which they are ready to part with and which they will give in addition to the money they can pay. Would it interest me to buy the picture from him (Matisse) and then sell it to these people, accepting the small Gauguin as a large part of the payment? I agreed, and it was thus that I met Michael and Sarah Stein, who then lived on the Rue Madame, over a kind of chapel. At their apartment I saw Leo and Gertrude. I recognized them as two people I had noticed at all the exhibitions and whose manner of dress had struck me as it did everyone then. Their costumes of corduroy and their sandals used to astonish the *habitués* of the Salons. I went to the Rue de Fleurus to visit Gertrude and Leo. Let me say that from that time all my fellow-feeling was for Gertrude, in whom, more and more, I found the 'great man' of the family. Her calm certitude impressed me far more than Leo's trenchant affirmations, for the latter often changed, bearing witness to a basic instability. A little later I became acquainted with Alice Toklas, whose intelligence and culture I gradually discovered in spite of an extraordinary modesty which sought only to hide them. I became a friend of Gertrude and Alice, and our friendship grew with each meeting.

Then Gertrude and Leo separated and divided the pictures. At their request, I made an estimate of the value of the Picassos and then acquired several which they wanted to sell, including a very large painting of the so-called 'Negro' period, *Trois femmes*, which Serge Schukin later purchased. Gertrude kept the other Picassos as her share. Thereafter I saw Leo occasionally, but Gertrude and Alice more and more often. Gertrude was among the first to admire and support our beloved Juan Gris. Then came the first world war.

I didn't see Gertrude again until 1920. Our meetings grew more frequent. We – my wife and I – dined often at 27 Rue de Fleurus. Gertrude and Alice came to see us in Boulogne; they were present several times at the Sunday gatherings when all our friends assembled around Juan Gris, our neighbor.

I remember one evening at the Rue de Fleurus. We had just finished dinner. The guests, besides my wife and me, included, I think, my wife's sister Béro and her husband Élie Lascaux. We were in the atelier, in the midst of wonderful pictures by Cézanne, Picasso, and Gris, when suddenly a cloud of thick smoke from the fireplace began to fill the room. A fire had broken out in the chimney. An emergency call was put in for the firemen, and they, the concierge, and the police all came rushing into the room. I can still see Gertrude's fine Roman head, impassive in the midst of the tumult, while the pebbles (which had been thrown from the roof down the flue to smother the fire) tumbled down onto the hearth with a sound like hail. At last everything grew quiet, and Gertrude went on talking as if nothing had happened.

She had had for a long time an old Ford, purchased just after the first war, which she called Godiva. I saw her once, perched high up on the front seat with Alice Toklas beside her, driving down the avenue des Champs-Elysées in this strange vehicle, very distinguished among the rush of quite different, lesser cars, paying no attention to the jokes and laughs of the crowd.

Doubtless I had soon found out that Gertrude Stein was a writer and not merely a collector of paintings. It seems to me that the first two pieces of her writing which I had occasion to read were the portraits of Matisse and Picasso, published by the courageous Stieglitz in 1912. I shall admit frankly that I did not at once understand these articles, but I was deeply impressed by them. An awareness of being confronted by something of great importance – that is what I felt. Then came the shock of the poetry, and at last a comprehension of the meaning. Let me say that this meaning appears to me today more than ever to constitute the most lucid portrait of these two painters. The *Leitmotiv* of the 'Picasso' for example – the 'This one was working' – strikes truly at the crux of the problem of the man and the painter Picasso, who lives only in order to work and is unhappy when he is not working.

It was after the first war that I read other works by Gertrude Stein, either printed in periodicals or in manuscript, and it was then that I conceived the idea of publishing something by her. As it happened I had the good fortune to carry out this plan.

Meanwhile other works appeared, the most important of them being *The Making of Americans*. This book I read with enthusiasm, not only savoring its value as literature but deeply moved by the story, notably – to cite but one example – by the wonderfully touching description of the departure of the family from their native city in Europe.

Why did I wish to publish Gertrude's work? The reason was that I believed I found in her writings a state of mind and aspirations which I had been defending for years. I have always thought that the quality in a period which really matters is never isolated but is reflected in thoughts which, although they are ignored by the majority, constitute the principal motive power for the life of the spirit of the time. Now Gertrude's poetry seemed to me very close to the painting of Picasso and Juan Gris, and, in another field, to the music of Schönberg. There was in it for me a manifestation, through language, of the same tendencies which had been made way for in Cubism, in plastic art. There was the same revolution in profundity, the same raising again of the problem of what makes the raw material of each art. In Gertrude's case it was a question of language, or more exactly of English vocabulary. The poetry with her comes from an entirely new use of this vocabulary, no longer accepting any law antecedent to the act of creation but freeing this act and leaving it abandoned to its interior logic. I have already cited elsewhere[1] a sentence of Gertrude's which is one of her most revealing: 'I like the feeling of words doing as they want to do and as they have to do.'

With Gertrude, we really have '*mots en liberté*,' while with Marinetti, the inventor of this phrase, the expressionistic use of the vocabulary is just the opposite of a freeing of words. That which appears to me also to bring Gertrude near to the Cubists is her use of the simplest words. The Cubists, on their part, had taken the most stripped forms to express the most ordinary objects, commonplace like the words which Gertrude used, never rare, her art in this respect differing completely from that of James Joyce. She was doubtless motivated by the same reasons that caused the Cubist painters to choose as subjects plates, bowls, fruit dishes, and then musical instruments, which they represented by forms which seemed geometric to spectators of that time – reasons which made the French poets called Cubists search equally for an extreme simplicity of vocabulary (for instance, Apollinaire in the works produced toward the end of his life, Max Jacob, and Pierre Reverdy). In this is to be seen, among other elements, a reaction against affectation, against the aesthetic character of the Symbolist generation.

It is important to understand that in Gertrude's work as in that of the Cubists we are dealing, in spite of appearances, with a realistic art, an art full of naturalness, of simplicity. The American writers of the period preceding hers of whom Gertrude spoke with sympathy and admiration were men like William Dean Howells and Mark Twain. And what was her first book? *Three Lives!*

What the Cubists knew, what Gertrude Stein knew, was that the

---

1. Daniel-Henry Kahnweiler, *Juan Gris: Sa Vie, Son Œuvre, Ses Écrits* (Paris, Gallimard, 1946), p.261.

work of art is not an imitation of something else but exists by itself, while *signifying* something else. The work of art, to exist, must preserve its unity. It was to this aim that the struggles of the Cubist painters, like those of Gertrude Stein, were directed. She stated it clearly in her lecture 'Composition as Explanation.' The title by itself is revealing, but I shall cite another particularly striking sentence: 'That started me into composing anything into one thing.' One could not express more plainly and more briefly the heart of the matter for our generation.

It was in 1924 that definite projects for publication were formulated. There was for one thing 'The Gertrude Stein Birthday Book,' which Gertrude had written for Picasso's son, Paul, and which I planned to publish with etchings by Picasso, printed like a real Birthday Book, each day carrying one sentence by Gertrude; and for another *A Book Concluding with 'As a Wife Has a Cow A Love Story'* which Juan Gris was to illustrate with lithographs. Gertrude speaks of these plans in her letters beginning in March of that year.[2] Unfortunately the first of these books never appeared. Why? I myself couldn't explain it exactly. Picasso had thought about it and had even engraved one plate containing four subjects which was to be cut for the separate printing of these four engravings. Obviously there would have had to be others. I wrote to Gertrude on 4 July 1925:

About the Birthday-Book, Picasso is to give us the engravings when he comes back from the South [he was at Juan-les-Pins, where I was to spend the month of August as his neighbor] and I don't think that 'a period of unreliability' is to interfere. I hope to issue the book at the end of the year.[3]

2. See Carl Van Vechten's letters to her of 5 March and 18 April 1924, printed in Donald Gallup, ed., *The Flowers of Friendship* (New York, Knopf, 1953), pp.159–60, 172.
3. *Op. cit.*, p.177.

Unfortunately I was mistaken in my optimism. Picasso's passive resistance – a term which seems to me more apt than Gertrude's 'period of unreliability,' resistance which shows itself in him, perhaps unconsciously, when he is faced by any commission, any work not spontaneously born of his own spirit but brought to him from outside – caused the failure of our project. In 1926 it was necessary to face the facts and give up plans for a book of which I should have been proud.

In contrast, the plan for the book illustrated by Gris was carried out. On 10 March 1926 Gris wrote me from Toulon:[4]

Gertrude Stein, who has just sent me a postcard, wants to know what happened to her book. I shall try to bring her at least the design for the coloured lithograph when I return.

On 26 March 1926 he wrote to Gertrude, still from Toulon:

I have made the design for the lithograph for your book.[5] It is in two colours, vivid red and black. Having tried several colours, with a figure and a landscape as a subject, I gave them all up in the end because it looked too horrible – a sort of a Camembert label in all its vulgarity. Now with a small still-life it looks quite like a label and is not bad at all. I have also made a sketch for a lithograph in black with a figure in case you want to put something at the beginning of the book.[6] I'll show them to you as soon as I'm back.

On 24 July 1926, from Boulogne-sur-Seine, where he had returned:

4. The quotations from Gris' letters are taken from the unpublished 'Juan Gris: Letters, 1913–1927'; ed. Daniel-Henry Kahnweiler, translated into English by Douglas Cooper. The originals of the letters from Gris to Gertrude Stein are in the Yale University Library.

5. Only one of the lithographs in the book is in color; the others are in black.

6. This lithograph, depicting a woman with a book, was used.

I am going to transfer the lithographs for your book on to stones in the next few days – the book is being printed. Send me your new address so that I can send you proofs of the lithographs as soon as I have them.

On 2 August 1926, also from Boulogne:

Kahnweiler comes back at the beginning of September. I don't think you can have proofs of your text before then. I will see about the lithographs myself as soon as I can walk again. I have a swollen foot as the result of injuring it here in the house a fortnight ago – it won't heal. With my bandaged foot I look like a gouty old gentleman.

On 8 September 1926, still from Boulogne:

With all this happening last month I haven't done a thing, and what's worse I am still beset with laziness. . . . In any case Kahnweiler, who reopened his gallery here three days ago, is going to bring me lithographic stones so that I can at last do the illustrations.

On 15 September 1926 (Boulogne):

I have no objection to your dedicating the book to Julia Ford. I am even delighted because you know I rather like [her father, Ford Madox] Ford in spite of all his eccentricities. But there is a sentence at the end of your letter which I have some difficulty in understanding. I don't know whether you want me to write the dedication to Julia F. on the lithograph or whether it is to be printed.[7] Will you please let me know about this because I am going to do the lithographs in the next few days?

7. It was to be printed.

Introduction to *Painted Lace*

On 24 October 1926 (Boulogne):

> I think the book must be ready by now and so we shall soon have
> to sign the numbered copies. They are all desperately slow.

And finally, on 28 November 1926, from Hyères, where he had just
gone, already ill:

> I am anxiously waiting for the book, which must now have ap-
> peared or at any rate must be on the point of doing so.

The book at last appeared, and Gertrude and Gris were satisfied
with it. Gris, more and more gravely ill, left Hyères for Puget-Theniers,
where he stayed only a few days. He returned to Paris almost dying,
grew better again, but succumbed to a third crisis of uremia on 11 May
1927. We were all grief-stricken. In memory of the friend we had lost,
Gertrude wrote 'The Life and Death of Juan Gris,' a heart-rending
elegy in which all three of our names are united.

When we lose a loved being it seems to us that life must stop; but it
goes on implacably. A new project for a book came into being. It was
'A Village Are You Ready Yet Not Yet,' which my brother-in-law Élie
Lascaux was to illustrate with lithographs. Gertrude had always liked
Lascaux's work; it was for that reason that I asked her for a manuscript
and she sent me 'A Village.' I replied on 1 December 1927:

> Many thanks for your kind letter. I wrote you at once, after re-
> ceiving the Ms, thanking you, and telling you that I liked it very
> much. Unfortunately it seems that my letter didn't arrive.
>
> Since, I have been reading the Ms again, and I like it still
> the more. I told Lascaux about it. I am very glad to publish it,
> and he, to illustrate it. I am going to translate it to him – that
> is not easy – and, afterwards, perhaps, we could talk the matter

over with Lascaux at Boulogne, spending an evening together. We could publish, then, the book at once.[8]

I am quite sure that Gertrude had chosen this text to fit her conception of Lascaux. Ten years later she wrote an exquisite preface for an exhibition of Lascaux's work at the Arts Club of Chicago, in which the title of the book – *A Village* – occurs repeatedly. Here is the conclusion of that preface:

> His painting has a white light that is a light and anything a village, green trees any part of Paris, Bourges, all and any french thing can be in that white light which is the light that Élie Lascaux has inside him.

A Village was the last of Gertrude Stein's works that I published. The economic crisis broke upon the world and I was not able to resume the publishing of books until many years later, being obliged to limit myself to my principal profession, that of dealer in pictures, for it was becoming extremely difficult to keep alive the artists who had placed their trust in me. Nevertheless our ties of friendship with Gertrude and Alice Toklas only tightened. We used to see each other frequently in Paris and in Bilignin as well. They had established themselves there in a charming house, after having spent several summers in the vicinity at the Hôtel Pernollet at Belley. Gertrude, as always, had set her stamp upon her dwelling-place. The fine garden on the terrace, cultivated by Alice, made a contrast to the mountain, rising harsh and rugged opposite.

Gertrude and Alice were at Bilignin when the second world war broke out. I was in Paris. One autumn day I received a telephone call from them. They had just arrived in Paris in order to take some pictures back to Bilignin and they wanted to return there as soon as

8. *The Flowers of Friendship*, p.213. The original of this letter is in the Yale University Library.

possible. They had left the rue de Fleurus some time before and were living in a ravishing eighteenth-century apartment at 5, rue Christine, a building of shabby appearance. I hurried there. Entering, I saw Alice with one foot on the frame of the portrait of Madame Cézanne, trying to remove the picture. I stopped her, and set myself to unframing this magnificent work in a less violent manner. They wanted to carry away with them only this picture and the portrait of Gertrude by Picasso, despite my protestations that they should take at least some small Picassos, which would be very easy to wrap and would take up very little room. A happy Providence justified their confidence. The pictures left in Paris survived.

I stored the two paintings in their car – Godiva had long since disappeared – and they left at once, having a permit for only a very short period. Being then in the southern zone, we kept in touch through letters even after the débâcle, until the moment when, with the zone occupied, it was necessary for all of us – Gertrude and Alice and my wife and I – to live '*dans la clandestinité*,' as it was called. We met again in Paris after the liberation. Then my wife died, and Gertrude and Alice climbed the four flights of stairs to bid her a last farewell. I cannot say that I suspected the existence of the illness which was wasting Gertrude away, but I remember that this visit touched me very much, for it seemed to represent a great effort for her.

At the end of July 1946, only a little more than a year after the death of my wife, I was at Cambridge visiting my sister. It was through an English newspaper, and not until two days after Gertrude's death, that I learned the terrible news for which I was not in the least prepared. Gertrude rests in the cemetery of Père Lachaise, not far from my wife's tomb, which will one day be also my own.

(Translated by Donald Gallup from the French)

NATALIE CLIFFORD BARNEY

Born in 1877 in Dayton, Ohio, Natalie Clifford Barney, heiress to a family fortune, fled to Europe in the early 1900s. Like Stein, who rejected the 'uncompromising family likeness' of American women – their 'conformity from within out' – Miss Barney was singularly uncomfortable in her homeland. 'Yes the American girl is a crude virgin and she is safe in her freedom,' Stein observed, concurring with Natalie Barney's scorn for her contemporaries.

In a three-hundred-year-old mansion on the rue Jacob, Miss Barney's salon rivaled Stein's in glamor. Paul Valéry, Colette, Remy de Gourmont were among the many who partook of the elegant chocolate cakes and fine liqueurs. At her frequent celebrations honoring *femmes de lettres* entertainment ranged from dramatic readings to startling spectacles. A bejeweled Mata Hari rode seminude through the garden and danced, fully naked, at a gathering for women only. After her morning horseback rides through the Bois de Boulogne, Miss Barney often assembled her friends in the garden's Grecian temple for a gracious tea.

Her salon was characterized by what Samuel Putnam called 'dignified *abandon*,' and the hostess herself was its most extraordinary figure. 'She was charming,' wrote Sylvia Beach, 'and, all dressed in white and with her blond coloring, most attractive. Many of her sex found her fatally so, I believe.'

Miss Barney made no attempt to conceal her lesbianism. Her flamboyant love affairs scandalized some, amused many, and inspired Sapphic poets and novelists.

A lifelong exile, Miss Barney became increasingly Parisian as the years passed. She wrote almost exclusively in French, recording her memories in five volumes spanning more than fifty years. Here she recalls the warmth and affection she felt for Gertrude Stein.

Foreword to
As Fine As Melanctha

In recalling so magnetic a personality, how not, first of all, evoke this magnet to which so many adhered? For she attracted and influenced not only writers but painters, musicians, and least but not last, disciples. She used to declare 'I don't mind meeting anyone once,' but she rarely kept to so strict a limitation. Although the most affirmative person I ever met, she was a keen and responsive listener.

'Life is as others spoil it for us,' concluded a beautiful friend of mine who had become a derelict through her fatalism. How many spoilt lives came to Gertrude with their misfortunes, due to some inextricable situation or sentimental rut? She, instead of offering helpless sympathy, often helped them out, by changing an *idée fixe* or obsession into a fresh start in a new direction.

As an appreciative pupil of William James, her study in reactions also proved salutary to the 'spoilers' of lives. In these she sometimes detected a genius for deceit which she would aid them to confess, or she would indicate means to liberate them of their victims, since as Henry James – was it not? – wisely remarked, 'There is only one thing worse than a tyrant and that is a tyrant's victim.'

Even more interested in cases than in their cures, many served as

From *As Fine As Melanctha* by Gertrude Stein (New Haven: Yale University Press, 1954), foreword by Natalie Barney. © 1954 by Yale University Press, reprinted by permission.

characters in her plays and stories. Some of them may even discover themselves in this very book . . . that is, if they are sufficiently initiated into Miss Stein's game of blindman's buff, or blindman's bluff, in which the reader is blindfolded – obscurity being the better part of discretion as to who is who. At other times she issued works of a most penetrating and acute quality, filled with subtle analysis, like

THINGS AS THEY ARE

Even I, who am not in the habit of consulting anybody about my dilemmas, once brought a problem of mine to the willing and experienced ear of Gertrude. In a moment, in a word, she diagnosed the complaint: 'Consanguinity.'

She never appeared to hesitate or reflect or take aim, but invariably hit the mark.

OUR WALKS

Often in the evening we would walk together; I, greeted at the door of 5 rue Christine by Gertrude's staunch presence, pleasant touch of hand, well-rounded voice always ready to chuckle. Our talks and walks led us far from war paths. For generally having no axe to grind nor anyone to execute with it, we felt detached and free to wander in our quiet old quarter where, while exercising her poodle, 'Basket,' we naturally fell into thought and step. Basket, unleashed, ran ahead, a white blur, the ghost of a dog in the moonlit side streets:

> Where ghosts and shadows mingle –
> As lovers, lost when single,

The night's enchantment made our conversation as light, iridescent and bouncing as soap bubbles, but as easily exploded when touched upon – so I'll touch on none of them for you, that a bubble may remain a bubble! And perhaps we never said *'d'impérissables choses.'*[1]

We also met during Gertrude Stein's lionized winter of 1934–35 in New York, and walked into one of its flashing, diamond-sharp days, where what one touches brings a spark to the finger tips.

Witnessing with apprehension Gertrude's independent crossing of streets without a qualm, I asked her why she never wavered on the edge of curbstones, as I did, with one foot forward and one foot backward, waiting for a propitious crowd and signal.

'All these people, including the nice taxi drivers, recognize and are careful of me.' So saying, she set forth, her longish skirt flapping sail-like in a sea breeze, and landed across 59th Street in the park, as confidently as the Israelites over the isthmus of the Red Sea – while we, not daring to follow in her wake, risked being engulfed.

She accepted her fame as a tribute, long on the way but due, and enjoyed it thoroughly. Only once, in Paris – and indeed the last time I saw her – did the recognition of a cameraman displease her, for he waylaid her just as we were entering Rumpelmayer's patisserie. In order to satisfy her need for the cake, and the photographer's wish, she was photographed by him, through the plate-glass window, eating the chosen one. Her eagerness was partly caused by a disappointing lunch we had just experienced at Prunier's, where each sort of sea food we ordered – prompted by appetites accrued by our recent war-time privations and still existing restrictions – was denied us, until at last (this was in 1946), driven to despair of a bettered world, Gertrude dropped her head between her hands and shook it from side to side; and not until we reached that rue de Rivoli patisserie did her spirits and appetite revive and meet with a partial compensation.

1. Baudelaire.

Foreword to *As Fine As Melanctha*

THEIR CAKES

The discovery of cakes had always been a peacetime pursuit of Gertrude and Alice. Meeting them by chance at Aix-le-Bains, I enquired why they happened to be on this opposite bank of the Lac du Bourget, and was informed of a new sort of cake created in one of the villages on a mountain beyond. But first obliged to go on other errands, they descended from the lofty seat of their old Ford car – Alice bejeweled as an idol and Gertrude with the air of an Indian divinity. As they disappeared around a corner, not without causing wonderment, the only appropriate offering seemed to me one of those long, hose-stemmed lotus flowers of dark pink, which I purchased and stuck between the spokes of Gertrude's steering wheel, with a card of explanation: 'A wand to lead you on.'

Another meeting with this inseparable couple took place in their *jardin de cure* at Bilignin, on another summer afternoon. It somewhat resembled the dust jacket Cecil Beaton designed for Gertrude Stein's *Wars I Have Seen,* only a huge parasol replaced the parachutes and we sat peacefully on gaily striped canvas chairs. The four of us – for Romaine Brooks had come along with me – and Basket, all curves and capers, lent a circus effect to the scene. As China tea was being served, Alice placed on the round outdoor table a fluffy confection of hers, probably a coconut layer cake which only Americans know how to make – and eat. Its white icing, edged with ornamental pink, matched Basket's like coating and incidental pinks. Gertrude sat in the favorite position in which Picasso portrayed her, clothed in rough attire, with moccasined feet, knees far apart, reminiscent of the gypsy-queen under her tent in my old Bar Harbor days.

Meanwhile Romaine, contemplating our group and finding it 'paintable,' wished to start a picture of it then and there, before the light or her inspiration should fade. But I, the disturbing element of the party, because of a clock in my mind and in duty bound to pleasures, insisted that Romaine and I were due elsewhere. So this picture of us was left unpainted: *mea culpa!*

Gertrude's and Alice's flair for cakes makes me conclude that while poets are left to starve in garrets – or, as here in France, in *chambres de bonnes* – living only in the past and future, with the hope of an aftermath of fame, an author such as Gertrude Stein, admitting of nothing but a 'continuous present,' must be sustained on sweetmeats and timely success, this being the surest way of taking the cake and of eating and having it too.

FAITH IN HERSELF

Her belief in herself never failed her. Even when still a child, she and her brother Leo used to discuss who would prove to be their family's genius. Leo thought himself that predestined genius; but Gertrude, turning to us – her two visitors were that afternoon Madame de Clermont-Tonnerre and myself – emphatically declared: 'But, as you know, it turned out to be me!'

Indeed, such a faith in oneself 'passeth understanding,' and what a poor thing is understanding, compared to such a faith!

As faith is far more exalting than reason, she once deplored Ezra Pound's becoming 'the village explainer,' which led so great a poet, and discoverer of poets, to his present standstill.

HER LECTURE AT OXFORD

From the crest of Gertrude Stein's tidal wave of success, she was persuaded by Harold Acton to lecture to a class of students at Oxford University, and she managed to hold them spellbound without a single concession to meet their understanding. Her lecture soared above their heads as they sensed something that surpassed them, but which freed neither their laughter nor their judgment, so that nothing was left to them but to applaud uproariously.

Foreword to *As Fine As Melanctha*

She afterwards consented to meet them on their level and both their questions and her answers were reported, inspiring and inspired.

WITH OUR G.I.s

This same democratic spirit made her popular with our G.I.s of the Second World War. They also gathered something unique from her presence amongst them, and so she led them, as a sort of *vivandière de l'esprit,* from war into peace, and to realize their own, instead of their collective, existence. But in some cases this change was hard to bring about, loath as they were to be 'separated from,' no longer 'club together, be part of, belong to,' etc. This fact was brought even to my notice in Florence by a big G.I. who confessed to me that 'the urge to join his comrades was so strong he couldn't even stop a moment to brush his teeth'! The disbanding of the herd instinct – to rebecome individual and perhaps a nobody instead of a company, to be left to the responsibility of oneself instead of leaving it to a chief in command with everything settled for you (death included), to take off a uniform to become uniform – all this was more than some of them could stand.

And how not to feel homesick for their regiment when forced homeward, perhaps to intrude on a family, or face hostile businessmen? At such a moment Gertrude Stein met them with her invigorating affirmations and cheered them on.

It must have been about this period that she was photographed against our Stars and Stripes.

BECOMING SINGULAR

Patriotic as Gertrude Stein seemed, she certainly dispelled our discouraging axiom that 'one man's as good as another.' No one has ever dared to say this of the American woman!

From her *Making of Americans,* I translated into French some of her

35

most significant pages on our 'progress in becoming singular.' These pages were read – between wars – in my salon, at meetings destined to bring about a better *entente* between French, English, and American authors.

On my 'Friday' celebrating Gertrude Stein, Mina Loy addressed them by explaining her admiration for this innovator who 'swept the literary circus clear for future performances.'

Many examples, including her own, were read to this effect – and a zeal for translating seized upon many of us from then on.

My *Aventures de L'esprit*, published in 1929, mentions these reunions as well as my literary adventures, including letters to me from Pierre Louys, Gabriel d'Annunzio, Marcel Proust, Rilke, Max Jacob, Paul Valéry, etc. This book Gertrude wanted to see translated for America, for it gives an incomplete but authentic résumé of our best period, and of those who made it so – and Gertrude Stein was included in this period and the forming of her own. How she stood her ground, never (unless to influence or appreciate) infringing on the ground of others. Indeed she made no allowances that 'he who runs may read,' and was heedless whether, having read, he ran.

We doubt if she ever thought of her readers at all.

In going over my impressions of her – *de vive voix, de vive mémoire* – in these fragmentary evidences, I find that I have somewhat replaced the essential by the superficial. I suppose that to want to enjoy and know such a personage without going into her more original ambitions and works is like seizing chance reflections from a water-mirror regardless of its depth; this is what I find myself doing here, and avoiding the significance of her undersea mysteries. Yet I have tried to dive deeper, and only touched rock bottom to be ejected up again to the surface, suffocating with too much salt water, in search of too rare a pearl.

CARL VAN VECHTEN

Gertrude Stein first glimpsed Carl Van Vechten at the second performance of Stravinsky's *Sacre du Printemps,* in 1913. He was 'a tall well built young man,' she noted, 'and he wore a soft evening shirt with the tiniest pleats all over the front of it.' Struck by his elegant appearance, she returned home and immediately wrote a portrait of him called, simply, 'One.'

Van Vechten was equally impressed a few days later when he called on Gertrude Stein at her home. Of all her admirers, he was the one who most directly led her to fame, and she acknowledged his role in *The Autobiography of Alice B. Toklas:*

> In season and out he kept her name and her work before the public. When he was beginning to be well known and they asked him what he thought the most important book of the year he replied *Three Lives* by Gertrude Stein. His loyalty and his effort never weakened.

He was born in Cedar Rapids, Iowa, in 1880. 'You are brilliant and subtle if you come from Iowa,' Gertrude Stein remarked. But for Van Vechten, Iowa offered nothing but bland middle-class complacency; he escaped as early as he could, enrolling at the University of Chicago and staying on in the city after he graduated in 1903. For the next three years he held a minor job on the staff of the *Chicago American,* spending as much time as he could in the city's theaters and concert

Carl Van Vechten, Portrait of Gertrude Stein (1934). Courtesy of The Estate of Carl Van Vechten.

halls. Although Chicago was a step beyond Cedar Rapids, it was not New York. In the spring of 1906 he headed East.

His career as a writer on the arts began with a position as assistant music critic for the *New York Times,* and he approached the task with tireless enthusiasm. He was writing for the *New York Press* and contributing to the *Trend* (where this selection originally appeared) when he met Stein during a visit to Paris. By 1922 he had turned novelist, fictionalizing his experiences in Paris and Greenwich Village in *Peter Whiffle: His Life and Works,* which received praise from Elinor Wylie, Carl Van Doren – and of course Stein – and sold surprisingly well.

Throughout his years as a writer Van Vechten spurred the acceptance of such novelists as Faulkner and Ronald Firbank, then considered avant-garde. He was among the first established critics to recognize the renaissance in African American arts and literature that was flourishing in Harlem, and he actively helped to establish the careers of Countee Cullen, Langston Hughes, James Weldon Johnson, Bessie Smith, and Ethel Waters.

Though much of his writing on African American arts appeared in *Vanity Fair,* he attempted a larger statement – one he hoped would bring the races closer together – in a novel he unfortunately titled *Nigger Heaven.* Gertrude Stein wrote enthusiastically that she found it 'delicate and real. . . . I am awfully pleased that it is so good.' She shared his belief that the only 'pioneering' being done in the United States was being done by African Americans. But others were not as kind as she. The book was attacked by whites and African Americans alike, stirring up passions Van Vechten had not foreseen.

Yet the novel did not diminish his stature as a critic, and his efforts on behalf of Gertrude Stein continued to be taken seriously. He acted as her agent in the United States, persuading Bennett Cerf that Random House should become her exclusive U.S. publisher. He arranged her 1934 lecture tour, attending to every detail for her comfort. He met her boat, arranged for her hotel suite, accompanied her on her first flight (she wouldn't fly without him), and set up a small private lecture so she could get used to speaking before a group. Above all, he never failed in his support. She called him the Patriarch, and he replied, 'it makes me feel like Moses or Abraham, but I guess I did lead you into the Promised Land.'

Van Vechten capped his long career in the arts by turning from writing to photography. From 1932 on his subjects ranged from Robinson Jeffers to Edna St. Vincent Millay, Tallulah Bankhead to Thomas Mann. During Stein's tour he brought her to his 55th Street apartment in New York to do a portrait of her. According to Alice Toklas, he took hundreds of photographs of Stein.

Stein named Van Vechten her literary executor, asking that he arrange for all her works to be published eventually. With Thornton Wilder, he saw that her papers were deposited safely at Yale, and the seventh and final volume of her writing was published by Yale University Press in 1957 under his guidance.[1] 'I always wanted to be historical, from almost a baby on, I felt that way about it,' Stein admitted shortly before she died, 'and Carl was one of the earliest ones that made me be certain that I was going to be.'

1. Two additional volumes of previously uncollected material were published by Black Sparrow Press in 1974, both edited by Robert Bartlett Haas: *Reflection on the Atomic Bomb* and *How Writing Is Written*.

'How to Read Gertrude Stein'

What is there to say for Gertrude Stein that she does not say quite adequately for herself? Is it not clear that her effect is made on all her readers? True, the effect varies, but did two people ever feel the same about Beethoven's Ninth Symphony? Why, even at the present moment the *Evening Globe* is being bombarded with letters from people who prefer 'Put on Your Old Gray Bonnet' to the masterpiece of the Bonn composer. Yet Beethoven's Ninth Symphony, even in the people that it does not reach as a solace and a boon, stirs a vague unrest, a feeling of reproach or of discontent.

'There is an art that we do not understand.'

It seems unnecessary to go so far afield as Beethoven in the beginning of an article concerning Miss Stein's *Tender Buttons*. Perhaps it is sufficient to send forth at first the mere suggestion that Miss Stein has added enormously to the vagueness of the English language, and vagueness is a quality that belongs to the English language, just as buildings on the Riviera sigh to be painted white, so that in the glory of that Southern sun they may reflect a thousand colors.

The English language is a language of hypocrisy and evasion. How not to say a thing has been the problem of our writers from the earliest times. The extraordinary fluidity and even naïveté of French makes it

First published in *The Trend* (August 1914: 553–57). Reprinted by permission of the Estate of Carl Van Vechten.

possible for a writer in that language to babble like a child; de Maupassant is only possible in French, a language in which the phrase '*Je t'aime*' means everything. But what does 'I love you' mean in English? Donald Evans, one of our poets, has realized this peculiar quality of English and he is almost the first of the poets in English to say unsuspected and revolting things, because he so cleverly avoids saying them.

Miss Stein discovered the method before Mr. Evans. In fact his Patagonian Sonnets were an offshoot of her later manner, just as Miss Kenton's superb story, 'Nicknames,' derives its style from Miss Stein's *Three Lives*. She has really turned language into music, really made its sound more important than its sense. And she has suggested to the reader a thousand channels for his mind and sense to drift along, a thousand instead of a stupid only one.

Miss Stein has no explanations to offer regarding her work. I have often questioned her, but I have met with no satisfaction. She asks you to read. Her intimate connection with the studies of William James have been commented upon; some say 'the fringe of thought,' so frequently referred to by that writer, may dominate her working consciousness. Her method of work is unique. She usually writes in the morning, and she sets down the words as they come from her pen; they bubble, they flow; they surge through her brain and she sets them down. You may regard them as nonsense, but the fact remains that effective imitations of her style do not exist. John Reed tells me that, while he finds her stimulating and interesting, an entity, he feels compelled to regard her work as an offshoot, something that will not be concluded by followers. She lives and dies alone, a unique example of a strange art. It may be in place also to set down here the fact that once in answer to a question Miss Stein asserted that her art was for the printed page only; she never expects people to converse or exchange ideas in her style.

As a personality Gertrude Stein is unique. She is massive in physique, a Rabelaisian woman with a splendid thoughtful face; mind dominating her matter. Her velvet robes, mostly brown, and her carpet slippers associate themselves with her indoor appearance. To go out she belts herself, adds a walking staff, and a trim unmodish turban. This garb suffices for a shopping tour or a box party at the Opéra.

Paris is her abode. She settled there after Cambridge, and association with William James, Johns Hopkins and a study of medicine. Her orderly mind has captured the scientific facts of both psychology and physiology. And in Paris the early painters of the new era captured her heart and purse. She purchased the best of them, and now such examples as Picasso's *Acrobats* and early Matisses hang on her walls. There is also the really authoritative portrait of herself, painted by Pablo Picasso.

These two painters she lists among her great friends. And their influence, perhaps, decided her in her present mode of writing. Her pictures are numerous, and to many, who do not know of her as a writer, she is mentioned as the Miss Stein with the collection of postimpressionists. On Saturday nights during the winter one can secure a card of admission to the collection and people wander in and out the studio, while Miss Stein serves her dinner guests unconcernedly with after-dinner coffee. And conversation continues, strangely unhindered by the picture viewers.

Leo Stein happens in, when he is not in Florence, and I have a fancy that he prefers Florence to Paris. He is her brother, and their tastes in art are naturally antithetical. He believes in the painters of the 'third dimension,' the painters of atmosphere, and the space between objects, for thus he describes the impressionists, and he includes Peter Paul Rubens in this group. And his precise manner of grouping thought is strangely at odds with Miss Stein's piquant love of gossip, and with her strange undercurrents of ideas that pass from her through and about the place.

Mr. Stein's phrase 'Define what you mean by – ' is almost famous. It is well known wherever he appears. Last I saw him in the Piazza

Vittorio Emanuele. I sat at luncheon time on the terrace of the Giubbi Rossi with Mabel Dodge when he strode into view, sandals on his feet, a bundle over his shoulder, and carrying an alpenstock. He was on his way to the mountains, and, if I remember rightly, he asked me, in response to an invitation, to define what I meant by 'cocktail,' something singularly difficult to do in Italy.

Miss Stein's presence, as I have said before my parenthesis, is strangely dominant in these evenings and her clear deep voice, her very mellow laugh, the adjunct of an almost abnormal sense of humor and observation, remain very pleasant memories. At one time I saw her very frequently, but we talked little of her work, although we often read it.

Of all her books only *Tender Buttons*, the latest of them to appear, is generally procurable. Besides this I know of *Three Lives*, written in her early manner; *Portrait of Mabel Dodge at the Villa Curonia*, an internationally famous monograph, published privately in Florence, and never on sale. There is a very long autobiographical work, at present, I believe considerably longer than *Clarissa Harlowe*, which runs through her various changes of style. There are several plays, one about me, which Miss Stein very kindly entitled 'One.' These are very short and in her very late manner. Miss Florence Bradley wished to play them in America and she may have done so in Chicago. She is now on her way to China and she may play them there; but I have no record of performances. Miss Stein is most insistent that they be performed before they are printed, but she did allow Marsden Hartley to quote from a play about him as a foreword to his collection of pictures which was exhibited at that 'little place' of Mr. Stieglitz's at 291 Fifth Avenue. There are several other short portraits, and some sketches, one of shop girls in the Gallerie Lafayette in Paris which is particularly descriptive and amusing. These, I think, are Miss Stein's main contributions to her complete works.

In *Three Lives* Miss Stein attained at a bound an amount of literary facility which a writer might strive in vain for years to acquire. Simplicity is a quality one is born with, so far as literary style is concerned, and Miss Stein was born with that. But to it she added, in this work, a vivid note of reiteration, a fascinatingly complete sense of psychology and the workings of minds one on the other, which at least in 'Melanctha: Each as She May' reaches a state of perfection which might have satisfied such masters of craft as Turgenev, or Balzac, or Henry James.

Quotation from this book is difficult. I shall quote a very short paragraph to give a sense of the style, and to show that those who are afraid of this writer in her present form need not be afraid of *Three Lives*.

'Jeff did not like it very well these days, in his true feeling. He knew now very well Melanctha was not strong enough inside her to stand any more of his slow way of doing. And yet now he knew he was not honest in his feeling. Now he always had to show more to Melanctha than he was ever feeling. Now she made him go so fast, and he knew it was not real with his feeling, and yet he could not make her suffer so any more because he always was so slow with his feeling.'

The story, it may be added, is about Negroes, and it is as poignant in its material as it is in its use of it. The book was published by the Grafton Press in New York. I think it is now out of print, but stray copies may sometimes be secured from dealers in rare books.

The number of *Camera Work* for August, 1912, contains two articles by Miss Stein about her two friends, Henri Matisse and Pablo Picasso. To me they seem to bridge the period between *Three Lives* and *Portrait of Mabel Dodge at the Villa Curonia*.

These have been considerably quoted in derision by newspaper paragraphers, but they are admirable examples of the effect of reiteration and of intertwining of ideas and phrases in style. Here is a quotation:

'This one was one having always something being coming out of him, something having completely a real meaning. This one was one whom some were following. This one was one who was working. This one was one who was working and he was one needing this thing needing to be working so as to be one having some way of working. This one was one who was working.'

Portrait of Mabel Dodge at the Villa Curonia made a winter amusing for those who subscribed to the clipping bureaus. The redoubtable Romeike, whom Whistler mentions, was kept busy cutting out ideas of the scriveners in Oshkosh and Flatbush about Miss Stein. To those who know Mrs. Dodge the portrait may seem to be a true one; it has intention, that is even obvious to those who do not know what the intention is. There is nothing faint or pale about Miss Stein's authority. It is as complete in its way as the authority of Milton. You may not like the words, but you are forced to admit, after, perhaps, a struggle that no other words will do.

For the sake of the few benighted ones who have not had this work quoted to them I offer the following passage, which is quite as familiar, I should say, as Wordsworth's 'A primrose at the river's brim.'

'A bottle that has all the time to stand open is not so clearly shown when there is green colour there. This is not the only way to change it. A little raw potato and then all that softer does happen to show that there has been enough. It changes the expression.'

And now a discussion of *Tender Buttons* seems imminent. Donald Evans, who is responsible for its publication, says that it is the only book ever printed which contains absolutely no errors. I have not Miss Stein's authority for this statement. At any rate the effect on printers and proofreaders was tremendous. I believe that even yet some of them are suffering from brain storm. *Portrait of Mabel Dodge at the Villa Curonia*, was set up in Florence by compositors who, I believe, did not read English. So their trouble was less.

There are several theories extant relating to *Tender Buttons*. I may say that one I upheld stoutly for a few hours, that the entire book has a physical application, I have since rejected, at least in part. The three divisions which comprise the books in a way explain the title. They are 'Food; Objects; Rooms,' all things which fasten our lives together, and whose complications may be said to make them 'tender.'

The majestic rhythm of the prose in this book; the virtuosity with which Miss Stein intertwines her words, are qualities which strike the ear at once. And *Tender Buttons* benefits by reading aloud. Onomatopoeia, sound echoing sense, is a favorite figure of speech with Miss Stein; so is alliteration which is fatally fascinating when mingled with reiteration, and Miss Stein drops repeated words upon your brain with the effect of Chopin's B Minor Prelude, which is popularly supposed to represent the raindrops falling on the roof at Majorca on one of those George Sand days.

The mere sensuous effect of the words is irresistible and often as in the section labeled 'Eating,' or 'A Seltzer Bottle,' the mere pronunciation of words gives the effect of the act or the article. On the other hand, 'A Little Called Pauline,' seems to me perfect in the way of a pretty description, a Japanese print of a charming creature. 'Suppose an Eyes' is similarly a picture, but more postery.

It would seem to me that the inspiration offered to writers in this book was an enormous incentive to read it. What writer after reading *Tender Buttons* but would strive for a fresher phrase, a more perfect rhythmic prose? Gertrude Stein to me is one of the supreme stylists.

In case one is not delighted, amused, or appealed to in any way by the sensuous charm of her art then, of course, there is the sense to fall back on; the ideas expressed. Here one floats about vaguely for a key to describe how to tell what Miss Stein means. Her vagueness is innate and one of her most positive qualities. I have already said how much she adds to language by it. You may get the idea of it if you close your eyes and imagine yourself awaking from the influence of ether, as you gasp to recall some words or ideas, while new ones surge into your brain. A certain sleepy consciousness. Or you may read sense through the figures as they flit rapidly – almost word by word – through your brain. It is worthy of note that almost everyone tries to make sense out of Miss Stein just as everyone insists on making photographs out of drawings by Picabia, when the essential of his art is that he is getting away from the photographic.

And now for a few quotations from *Tender Buttons:*

'RED ROSES: A cool red rose and a pink cut pink, a collapse and a solid hole, a little less hot.'

'A SOUND: Elephant beaten with candy and little pops and chews all bolts and reckless reckless rats, this is this.'

Roast beef is Miss Stein's favorite food and she has devoted nearly seven pages in the section labeled 'Food' to its delights, while oranges and such-like are let off with single phrases. In the middle of the description of roast beef is a verse, discovered for me by Neith Boyce, which I print in verse form, although it is not disclosed in the book:

> Lovely snipe and tender turn,
> Excellent vapor and slender butter
> All the splinter and the trunk,
> All the poisonous darning drunk,
> All the joy in weak success,
> All the joyful tenderness,
> All the section and the tea,
> All the stouter symmetry.

Celery is thus described: 'Celery tastes tastes where in curled lashes and little bits and mostly in remains.'

'A green acre is so selfish and so pure and so enlivened.'

And the description of chicken has already become a byword among certain groups of those who love bywords:

'Alas a dirty word, alas a dirty third alas a dirty third, alas a dirty bird.'

SYLVIA BEACH

The daughter of a Presbyterian minister from Princeton, New Jersey, Sylvia Beach came to Paris in 1917 to pursue her interest in contemporary French writing. For a while she lived with her beautiful sister, Cyprian, an actress, in a 'fairly respectable' quarter near the Palais Royal. Her search for current literature soon brought her to *La Maison des Amis des Livres,* run by Adrienne Monnier. The bookshop was a popular rendezvous for French writers, a salon where hundreds gathered to listen to André Gide read the poems of Paul Valéry or hear Valéry Larbaud read his translation of *Ulysses,* or to attend an occasional musical program by Erik Satie or Francis Poulenc.

Miss Beach and Mlle. Monnier, sharing a love of literature, became close friends, making as odd a couple as Gertrude Stein and Alice Toklas. Large, buxom Mlle. Monnier, who reminded Virgil Thomson of 'a French milkmaid from the eighteenth century,' contrasted with Miss Beach's pert boyishness. 'Angular Sylvia, in her box-like suits, was Alice in Wonderland at forty,' Thomson recalled.

Sylvia Beach had long wanted to open a bookshop of her own, and now she began to plan a French shop in New York, where she could make known the works of the new French writers introduced to her by Adrienne Monnier. When it became apparent, however, that the costs of establishing a shop in the United States would be too high, she was forced to abandon her dream.

Mlle. Monnier, delighted to keep her friend in Paris, suggested that instead of a French bookstore in New York, she open an American shop near *La Maison des Amis des Livres*. Quickly convinced, Sylvia Beach sent a telegram to her mother in Princeton, saying simply: 'Opening bookshop in Paris. Please send money.' Mrs. Beach forwarded her entire savings.

On November 19, 1919, Shakespeare and Company took down its shutters for the first time. Photographs of Walt Whitman and Edgar Allan Poe hung beside two drawings by William Blake; some Whitman manuscripts – family heirlooms – were carefully displayed among the flea-market furnishings and the varied selection of English and American books. Within hours the first customers arrived – among them André Gide and André Maurois – and for more than twenty years, Miss Beach recalled, 'they never gave me time to meditate.'

Miss Beach's cheerful friendliness welcomed many newly arrived Americans to Paris. Hemingway remembered her 'lively, sharply sculptured face, brown eyes that were alive as a small animal's and as gay as a young girl's, and wavy brown hair.' She let him borrow books without paying the required rental fee, and often gently reminded him to eat. 'No one that I ever knew was nicer to me,' he said years later.

The shop served not only as a meeting place but even as a mailing address. Robert McAlmon's publishing house, Contact Editions, received manuscripts and orders c/o Shakespeare and Company, and it was a rare day that the blue-eyed young writer did not wander in once or twice. He was part of 'the Crowd,' the writers and artists whose portraits, photographed by Man Ray or Berenice Abbott, gradually filled the walls beside the Blake drawings.

Among Miss Beach's customers was James Joyce, who would borrow dozens of books and keep them for years. He sat quietly for hours at a time in the shadowy corner of the shop, emerging only rarely to be introduced to an aspiring writer. In 1922, Shakespeare and Company dared to publish his *Ulysses,* selling it by subscription throughout Europe and Great Britain and making literary history.

from *Shakespeare and Company*

Since Gertrude Stein's studio was just a few blocks from the rue de l'Odéon where Shakespeare and Company finally settled, she and Miss Toklas were frequent visitors. In turn, Sylvia Beach often brought young writers – Sherwood Anderson among them – to the rue de Fleurus to meet the legendary writer.

from *Shakespeare and Company*

Not long after I had opened my bookshop, two women came walking down the rue Dupuytren. One of them, with a very fine face, was stout, wore a long robe, and, on her head, a most becoming top of a basket. She was accompanied by a slim, dark, whimsical woman: she reminded me of a gipsy. They were Gertrude Stein and Alice B. Toklas.

Having been an early reader of *Tender Buttons* and *Three Lives*, I was, of course, very joyful over my new customers. And I enjoyed their continual banter. Gertrude was always teasing me about my bookselling, which appeared to amuse her considerably. It amused me, too.

Her remarks and those of Alice, which rounded them out, were inseparable. Obviously they saw things from the same angle, as people do when they are perfectly congenial. Their two characters, however, seemed to me quite independent of each other. Alice had a great deal more finesse than Gertrude. And she was grown up: Gertrude was a child, something of an infant prodigy.

Gertrude subscribed to my lending library, but complained that there were no amusing books in it. Where, she asked indignantly, were those American masterpieces *The Trail of the Lonesome Pine* and *A Girl of the Limberlost*? This was humiliating for the librarian. I produced the works of Gertrude Stein, all I had been able to lay my hands on at the time, and I wondered if she could mention another library in Paris that had two copies of *Tender Buttons* circulating. To make up for her unjust criticism of Shakespeare and Company, she bestowed several of her works on us: quite rare items such as *Portrait of Mabel Dodge at the Villa Curonia* and that thing with the terrifying title, *Have They Attacked Mary. He giggled. A Political Caricature.* Also the special number of the Stieglitz publication, *Camera Work,* containing her pieces on Picasso and Matisse. But, above all, I valued the copy of [*As Fine As*] *Melanctha* in the first edition, which Gertrude inscribed for me. I should have locked it up; someone stole it from the bookshop.

Gertrude's subscription was merely a friendly gesture. She took little interest, of course, in any but her own books. But she did write a poem about my bookshop, which she brought to me one day in 1920. It was entitled 'Rich and Poor in English' and bore the subtitle, 'to subscribe in French and other Latin Tongues.' You can find it in *Painted Lace,* Volume V of the Yale edition of her work.

I saw Gertrude and Alice often. Either they dropped in to observe my bookselling business or I went around to their *pavillon* in the rue de Fleurus near the Luxembourg Gardens. It was at the back of the court. Gertrude always lay stretched on a divan and always joked and teased. The *pavillon* was as fascinating as its occupants. On its walls were all those wonderful Picassos of the 'Blue period.' Also, Gertrude showed me the albums that contained his drawings, of which she had collected a good many. She told me that she and her brother Leo had agreed to divide between them all the pictures they possessed. He had chosen Matisse, she Picasso. I remember some paintings by Juan Gris, too.

Once, Gertrude and Alice took me for a ride into the country. They drove up noisily in the old Ford named Gody, a veteran of the war and companion in their war work. Gertrude showed me Gody's latest acquisitions – headlights that could be turned on and off at will from inside the car and an electric cigarette lighter. Gertrude smoked continuously. I climbed up on the high seat beside Gertrude and Alice, and off we roared to Mildred Aldrich's 'hilltop on the Marne.'

Gertrude did the driving, and presently, when a tire blew out, she did the mending. Very competently too, while Alice and I chatted by the roadside.

Gertrude Stein's admirers, until they had met her and discovered how affable she was, were often 'skeered' to approach her without proper protection. So the poor things would come to me, exactly as if I were a guide from one of the tourist agencies, and beg me to take them to see Gertrude Stein.

My tours, arranged with Gertrude and Alice beforehand, took place in the evenings. They were cheerfully endured by the ladies in the *pavillon,* who were always cordial and hospitable.

One of the first of these tourists was a young friend of mine who hung around Shakespeare and Company a great deal in 1919–20, Stephen Benét. He may be seen in one of the first press photos of the bookshop, that fellow peering through his glasses at a book and very serious-looking compared with my sister Holly and me in the back of the shop.

At his request, and on his own responsibility, I took Stephen to see Gertrude Stein. This was before his marriage to that charming Rosemary, whom he later brought to the bookshop. The visit to Gertrude went off pleasantly. I believe Stephen mentioned that he had some Spanish blood, and since Gertrude and Alice liked anything Spanish, that interested them. I don't think the meeting left any traces, however.

Another 'tourist' who asked me to take him around to the rue de Fleurus was Sherwood Anderson. One day I noticed an interesting-looking man lingering on the doorstep, his eye caught by a book in the window. The book was *Winesburg, Ohio,* which had recently been published in the United States. Presently he came in and introduced himself as the author. He said he hadn't seen another copy of his book in Paris. I was not surprised, as I had looked everywhere for it myself – in one place they had said, 'Anderson, Anderson? Oh, sorry, we have only the Fairy Tales.'

from *Shakespeare and Company*

Sherwood Anderson was full of something that had happened to him, a step he had taken, a decision he had made that was of the greatest importance in his life. I listened with suspense to the story of how he had suddenly abandoned his home and a prosperous paint business, had simply walked away one morning, shaking off forever the fetters of respectability and the burden of security.

Anderson was a man of great charm, and I became very fond of him. I saw him as a mixture of poet and evangelist (without the preaching), with perhaps a touch of the actor. Anyhow, he was a most interesting man. . . .

Sherwood told me that Gertrude Stein's writing had influenced him. He admired her immensely, and asked me if I would introduce him to her. I knew he needed no introduction, but I gladly consented to conduct him to the rue de Fleurus.

This meeting was something of an event. Sherwood's deference and the admiration he expressed for her writing pleased Gertrude immensely. She was visibly touched. Sherwood's wife, Tennessee, who had accompanied us, didn't fare so well. She tried in vain to take part in the interesting conversation between the two writers, but Alice held her off. I knew the rules and regulations about wives at Gertrude's. They couldn't be kept from coming, but Alice had strict orders to keep them out of the way while Gertrude conversed with the husbands. Tennessee was less tractable than most. She seated herself on a table ready to take part in the conversation, and resisted when Alice offered to show her something on the right side of the sitting room. But Tennessee never succeeded in hearing a word of what they were saying. I pitied the thwarted lady – I couldn't see the necessity for the cruelty to wives that was practiced in the rue de Fleurus. Still, I couldn't help being amused at Alice's wife-proof technique. Curiously, it was only applied to wives; non-wives were admitted to Gertrude's conversation.

Sherwood Anderson was judged harshly by the young writers; and suffered considerably from the falling-off of his followers. But he was a forerunner, and, whether they acknowledge it or not, the generation of the twenties owes him a considerable debt.

Gertrude Stein had so much charm that she could often, though not always, get away with the most monstrous absurdities, which she uttered with a certain childish malice. Her aim was usually to tease somebody; nothing amused her as much. Adrienne Monnier, whom I took around to Gertrude's once, didn't find her very amusing. 'You French,' Gertrude declared, 'have no Alps in literature, no Shakespeare; all your genius is in those speeches of the generals: fanfare. Such as *"On ne passera pas!"* '

I disagreed with Gertrude on French writing as well as on other writing, for instance, Joyce's. She was disappointed in me when I published *Ulysses;* she even came with Alice to my bookshop to announce that they had transferred their membership to the American Library on the Right Bank. I was sorry, of course, to lose two customers all of a sudden, but one mustn't coerce them. In the rue de l'Odéon, I must admit, we kept low company.

Thus 'The Flowers of Friendship Faded Friendship Faded,' at least for a time. But resentment fades as well. It's so difficult to remember exactly what a disagreement was all about. And there was Gertrude Stein's writing; nothing could affect my enjoyment of that.

After a while, I saw Gertrude and Alice again. They came to see whether I had anything by William Dean Howells, a major American writer, according to Gertrude, and unjustly neglected. I had his complete works, and made Gertrude and Alice take them all home.

Toward the end of 1930, I went one day with Joyce to a party at the studio of our friend Jo Davidson. Gertrude Stein, a fellow-bust of Joyce's, was also there. They had never met, so, with their mutual consent, I introduced them to each other and saw them shake hands quite peacefully.

Dear Jo Davidson! How we did miss him when he was gone.

The last time I took a 'skeered' person to see Gertrude was when

Ernest Hemingway told me he wanted to make up his quarrel with her but couldn't get up the courage to go alone. I encouraged him in his plan, and promised to accompany him to the rue Christine, where Gertrude and Alice were then living. I thought it better for Hemingway to go up alone, so I took him all the way to her door and left him with my best wishes. He came to tell me afterward that it was 'fine' between them again.

Wars between writers blaze up frequently, but I have observed that they settle down eventually into smudges.

SHERWOOD ANDERSON

In 1914, seven years before he met Gertrude Stein, Sherwood Anderson discovered her recently published volume, *Tender Buttons*, that slim collection of descriptions of such everyday objects as a box, a plate, a seltzer bottle, a book, an apple. But the descriptions themselves, far from ordinary, are whimsical, unexpected, and, to some, unintelligible. To Sherwood Anderson, *Tender Buttons* opened a new dimension in language.

> It excited me as one might grow excited in going in a new and wonderful country where everything is strange – a sort of Lewis and Clark expedition for me. Here words laid before me as the painter had laid the color pans on the table in my presence. My mind did a kind of jerking flop and after Miss Stein's book had come into my hands I spent days going about with a tablet of paper in my pocket and making new and strange combinations of words. The result was I thought a new familiarity with the words of my own vocabulary. I became a little conscious where before I had been unconscious. Perhaps it was then I really fell in love with words, wanted to give each word I used every chance to show itself at its best.[1]

Tender Buttons, as Anderson so aptly understood, 'was something purely experimental and dealing in words separated from sense – in

1. Sherwood Anderson, *A Story Teller's Story* (New York: Huebsch, 1924), p.362.

the ordinary meaning of the word sense – an approach I was sure the poets must often be compelled to make.' It was an approach he decided to try. He would aim, as Miss Stein explained in *Portraits and Repetition,* 'to express what something was, a little by talking and listening to that thing, but a great deal by looking at that thing.'

> A table, for her, took on a new aura:
> A table means does it not my dear it means a
> whole steadiness. Is it likely that a change.
>
> A table means more than a glass even a looking
> glass is tall. A table means necessary places and
> a revision a revision of a little thing it means it
> does mean that there has been a stand, a stand
> where it did shake.

Anderson, though, never took up Miss Stein's style. *Tender Buttons* and her other works, especially *Three Lives,* enabled him to find another kind of liberation. He wrote of Stein to his daughter-in-law in 1934:

> she taught me to recognize the second person in myself, the poet-writing person, so that I could occasionally release that one.
> And not blame it for the anxious person, myself as known by others.
> You can see the great gain in that to me and why I think Stein is a genius.[2]

When Sherwood Anderson finally arrived in Paris in 1921, he asked Sylvia Beach to arrange for him to visit Gertrude Stein in her rue de Fleurus studio, and, as Stein recalled, 'quite simply and directly as was his way told her what he thought of her work and what it had meant

2. Howard Mumford Jones, ed., *Letters of Sherwood Anderson* (Boston: Little, Brown, 1953), pp.300–301.

to him in his development.'[3] Other writers had taken Stein as mentor, absorbed what they would, and then, disappointingly for her, strayed in their loyalty and affection. But Anderson remained an outspoken defender of her art, acknowledging in print what he often expressed to her – his debt, his gratitude, his esteem.

'You always manage to say so much and say it straighter than anyone else I know,' he wrote of her comments on *A Story Teller's Story*, his autobiography. And he readily admitted, 'It was a vital day for me when I stumbled upon you.'[4]

Their friendship flourished for twenty years, until Anderson died in 1941, and with him the plans for a joint work on Ulysses S. Grant, their 'great American hero.' Their meetings were few: he rarely had enough money to travel to Paris; she came to the United States only once, for her lecture tour in 1934, and found him when he was traveling through Minnesota. Yet their correspondence reflected the mutual respect and appreciation which is evident in the selection that follows. Stein never failed in her praise of his work, declaring that 'except Sherwood there was no one in America who could write a clear and passionate sentence.'[5]

In his introduction to her collection *Geography and Plays*,[6] he wrote that 'there is in America an impression of Miss Stein's personality, not at all true and rather foolishly romantic . . . of . . . a languid woman lying on a couch, smoking cigarettes, sipping absinthes perhaps and looking out upon the world with tired, disdainful eyes.' In Gertrude Stein's Kitchen in 'Four American Impressions,' he does his best to dispel the myth and portray the woman he knew.

3. Gertrude Stein, *The Autobiography of Alice B. Toklas* (New York: Harcourt, Brace, 1933), p.241.

4. Ray Lewis White, ed., *Sherwood Anderson/Gertrude Stein: Correspondence and Personal Essays* (Chapel Hill: University of North Carolina Press, 1972), p.46.

5. Stein, *Toklas*, p.268.

6. Boston: Four Seas Company, 1922.

from Four American Impressions

One who thinks a great deal about people and what they are up to in the world comes inevitably in time to relate them to experiences connected with his own life. The round hard apples in this old orchard are the breasts of my beloved. The curved round hill in the distance is the body of my beloved, lying asleep. I cannot avoid practicing this trick of lifting people out of the spots on which in actual life they stand and transferring them to what seems at the moment some more fitting spot in the fanciful world.

And I get also a kind of aroma from people. They are green healthy growing things or they have begun to decay. There is something in this man, to whom I have just talked, that has sent me away from him smiling and in an odd way pleased with myself. Why has this other man, although his words were kindly and his deeds apparently good, spread a cloud over my sky?

In my own boyhood in an Ohio town I went about delivering newspapers at kitchen doors, and there were certain houses to which I went — old brick houses with immense old-fashioned kitchens — in which I loved to linger. On Saturday mornings I sometimes managed

First published in 'Four American Impressions: Gertrude Stein, Paul Rosenfeld, Ring Lardner, Sinclair Lewis,' *The New Republic* (11 October 1922: 171–73). Reprinted in *Gertrude Stein: A Composite Portrait*, edited by Linda Simon (New York: Avon Books, 1974), 71–73.

to collect a fragrant cooky at such a place but there was something else that held me. Something got into my mind connected with the great light kitchens and the women working in them that came sharply back when, last year, I went to visit an American woman, Miss Gertrude Stein, in her own large room in the house at 27 rue de Fleurus in Paris. In the great kitchen of my fanciful world in which, ever since that morning, I have seen Miss Stein standing there is a most sweet and gracious aroma. Along the walls are many shining pots and pans, and there are innumerable jars of fruits, jellies and preserves. Something is going on in the great room, for Miss Stein is a worker in words with the same loving touch in her strong fingers that was characteristic of the women of the kitchens of the brick houses in the town of my boyhood. She is an American woman of the old sort, one who cares for the handmade goodies and who scorns the factory-made foods, and in her own great kitchen she is making something with her materials, something sweet to the tongue and fragrant to the nostrils.

That her materials are the words of our English speech and that we do not, most of us, know or care too much what she is up to does not greatly matter to me. The impression I wish now to give you of her is of one very intent and earnest in a matter most of us have forgotten. She is laying word against word, relating sound to sound, feeling for the taste, the smell, the rhythm of the individual word. She is attempting to do something for the writers of our English speech that may be better understood after a time, and she is not in a hurry.

And I have always that picture of the woman in the great kitchen of words, standing there by a table, clean, strong, with red cheeks and sturdy legs, always quietly and smilingly at work. If her smile has in it something of the mystery, to the male at least, of the Mona Lisa, I remember that the women in the kitchens on the wintry mornings wore often that same smile.

She is making new, strange and to my ears sweet combinations of words. As an American writer I admire her because she, in her person, represents something sweet and healthy in our American life, and because I have a kind of undying faith that what she is up to in her word kitchen in Paris is of more importance to writers of English than the work of many of our more easily understood and more widely accepted word artists.

SAMUEL BARLOW

He was twenty-three, a sergeant in the Office of Military Intelligence in Marseille, when he was sent to Nimes to investigate a report that a certain hotel proprietor was behaving suspiciously. 'Somewhere at the end of the string,' recalled Samuel Barlow, 'was a Miss Stein.' When he boarded his train to Nimes, he did not realize that the Miss Stein he sought was the literary iconoclast Gertrude Stein, of whom he had heard much: 'I was not a complete yokel, yahoo, and ignoramus.'

Stein and Toklas treated Barlow to the kind of tour that they gave other young soldiers during the war years, when the distributed supplies in their Ford, christened 'Auntie.' When, for example, a young Amherst student, William Garland Rogers, found himself in the south of France, the two women insisted that he accompany them on some jaunts, serving as their mechanic-in-residence as well as their companion. Rogers agreed that they needed some help with 'Auntie,' a car that seemed totally collapsible, and, like Barlow, he was grateful for their company and attentions. As they toured together, Gertrude offered historical tidbits, Alice aesthetic judgments, food, and wine.

In this affectionate tribute to Stein and Toklas, Barlow offers not only a vivid recollection of his two new friends, but also a sensuous rendering of the countryside, its texture, light, fragrances, and rhythms. Whereas Rogers's memoir, *When This You See Remember Me,* has been mined most often by Stein's biographers, Barlow's offers a fresh perspective of this period of Stein's life.

Ave Dione

A Tribute

I had a letter to Gertrude Stein. It was six months before the Armistice, 1918. She was in Nimes, I was on leave in Marseille.

A local train carried me through the most fascinating, incredible hundred square miles of country in the world, into the heart of Provence. She made me love it; she, in one too-brief day, made it impossible for me not to go back in later years, time and again; she instructed my young mind. But on the train I boned up, also, with a good history.

Here was I leaving Marseille, the ancient republic. Iberian, Ligurian, Phoenician origins – my book was specific. Roscius, the delight of Nero, was born here (as are half the modern French stage-folk); Petronius, probably, too. If you peeled two thousand years off time's eyes, you could see the Greek villas and the illustrious exiles. Seneca, with first rate principles and second hand thoughts. And then, much too soon, I was walking to the hotel in Nimes in the dusk. About me in the air a classic smell of olive and cypress fagets [sic], onion, and September winepresses, and a fine mist rising from the canal which the Romans digged and which Le Notre, in a lace ruffle, revived.

At supper, Miss Stein put Provence squarely in the center of my map, forever. She said, 'If you are not, and I gather you are not, familiar with Provence, you should be. The soup here is good, the meat

From the Gertrude Stein Collection, Yale Collection of American Literature, Beinecke Rare Book and Manuscript Library, Yale University. Published by permission of the Yale University Library.

fair, but since we are less than a hundred miles from the sea the fish is poor. Otherwise not a bad hotel except for the proprietor. It is the hottest place in summer and the windiest in winter. It has fed (I don't mean the hotel, but Provence) the best painters of the last fifty years and it has had a continuous and lovely civilization for nearly two thousand. One of the Roman Emperors thought of leaving Rome to set his capitol here, and, later, the Popes had the luck. If a man wanted to breathe in the essence of Spain and Italy – of all that's Gallic, and most of roman Rome that's left, – all at a gulp before he died, – just once more, – I doubt if he could do better than lean out a window in Arles, or Nimes here, or Avignon. Curious that no one understands rice-pudding in France. . . .'

'You see,' said Miss Toklas, 'Miss Stein and I run an ambulance which distributes supplies to all the hospitals and rest-camps in these parts. We've had no shipment for two weeks and we are both itching for something to do. And, what's more, we have stored up the last two weeks' supply of gasoline: more precious than ointment or jewels.'

Miss Stein turned to Miss Toklas. 'I see no reason, my dear, why we should not Cook-tour this young man to our favorite spots, give him a day he'll never forget, and have ourselves a time. If you'll see to sandwiches?'

Then to me, 'Cézanne and Van Gogh and Laura, and, since you're musical, the troubadour who wrote *Le pommier doux*,' and the Marius (busy General) who named half the actual population, – well, their dust will blow down the road before us tomorrow, and it won't keep the Mistral out, either.

'Is seven o'clock too early?'

I was in the court-yard next morning when Miss Toklas appeared with the sandwiches and a bottle of wine. She showed me the ambulance –

a small, serviceable Ford camionette. We threw a couple of cushions and a soap box in the rear for me. Miss Stein arrived to take charge.

I had not properly observed her in the dining room the evening before; a portly and plain person of great charm: a grey bust arising over the table cloth. Now, – though her outfit was the same, – the full-length came as a surprise. It ended in bare feet and heavy, thonged sandals, one toe on each foot separated proudly from its fellows like the little pig who went to market. The rest of her massive figure was clothed in a monk's garment of sacking. Possibly sack-cloth, but the impression was cheerful if not garish. A head with greying hair pulled back into a bun, and fine, prehensile eyes. I think I remember her gaiety, her wise gaiety, best.

Miss Stein sat at the wheel; Miss Toklas beside her. I had the whole end of the camionette, framing the day like the door in The Walkure, to see from, or for surplus, by squatting, a few inches between the heads of my hostesses and the top. Mostly I squatted, to catch any guiding, pointing word that came from the front. The car rattled: I hit the sides; I peered around the corner of my door; I craned over their heads. But there was no such thing as discomfort. I capitulated only to splendor that day.

'The Grand Tour will commence here, since we're here,' said Miss Stein. And we chugged out of the hotel courtyard, across the square, skirting the Amphitheater, up the main street to the Maison Carres, that Tanagra among temples. 'No insides,' cried Miss Stein back to me. 'No time!'

Through the middle of marketing crowds, dodging the tied calf and the running dog, we drove to the gates of the Park. Here were Roman baths, fed from the deep spring, the colors of the copper-purple edge of oysters, that still flows out under the mountain. Here too Le Notre spanned the stream, raised balustrades with marble figures, correct, ridiculous, charming, – all to tempt the Grand Monarque to build in this place, at this halt on the way to the Spanish marriage, what later rose at Versailles. And up the face of the great hill, now almost covered with brambles, sprawl the stone terraces and flights of steps which were to lead to a palace. In place of the palace, the hill is crowned with the Tour Magne. Keep of Charlemagne? Eye of the Goths? Now like a huge wind-mill without paddles. Victor Hugo made a verse of it:

> Gal, amant de la reine, alla, tour magnanime,
> Galamant de l'arene a la Tour Magne a Nimes.

'I'd like one of the marble tubs the Romans used to have here,' said Miss Stein. 'I've seen one in the museum.'

'You know you'd wash the dog in it,' said Miss Toklas.

'What dog,' said Miss Stein to me, 'do you think would look best bathed in porphyry?'

'Time!' called Miss Toklas; and we returned to the Ford.

The road from Nimes to Aigues Mortes ran through the mane of a lion who had rolled in the grass. Tawny ridges and buttes, an occasional spire of cypress or smoke-puff of olive, or a fig-tree writhing like Laocoon. And always the tic's track of grey road. Once the sea, and then the Rhone, had pounded here and chiseled. The Goths probably knew Les Baux reflected in a lake; and St. Louis bathed near by in the sea. All trace is not gone, for half way from Nimes, southward, we struck the marshes and lagoons and rolling lands of the Camargue, where cattle are rounded up by a lean race of men in leather chaps, with red handkerchiefs at their throats, and who use the lasso. Tough customers, like our own cow-boys; and the girls dark with the blood of Arles and the legions of Marius.

We pulled to one side to let by a train of bullock-carts. Tan-gray beasts, pagan and grave, drawing carts piled with purple and green grapes. The juice spilled from the lip of the wagons; the men and women walked by the road-side, carrying the harvest equipment.

Ave Dione: A Tribute

Through the dust-cloud, as the crew passed, Ceres and Pomona, something instantly classic, stately, joyous, transfixed us for a moment.

'A mirage rather than vision,' said Miss Stein to Miss Toklas. 'There's more what we call paganism today than there was then. Real pagans were so conventional. If the cat sneezed you had to stay indoors all day, neglect the harvest, and give an obol to the priest. And no kissing on Sundays.'

We rounded a corner. 'There's Aigues Mortes,' cried Miss Toklas, 'that black glove with fingers in the air lying on its back in a sandpile.' A great square of gun-metal wall, throwing up dark towers, sat full in the plain. Once the sea had protected it on three sides, lapping the rake under the battlements and filled the moat. Ladies had waved from the turrets to the ships of a departing crusade, King Louis's galleon in the lead. Now, defenseless, unviolated by the restorers of Napoleon III, it rose more sinister, more striking than Carcassonne.

'More Froissard than Walter Scott, thank God,' said Miss Stein. 'Do you know Barres' "*Jardin de Berenice*"?'

We drove over a draw-bridge, through a black portal, into the half-deserted citadel. I forget everything except the walls, the site, – the heavy splendor of this iron crown, empty.

'It's best from the top of the towers. You can see the sea and the canal. And you get an idea of the defenses from up there. I'll go with you.'

Miss Toklas sprang out with me, and we climbed to the *chemin de ronde* and on up to the topmost parapet. The Ford was a speck, a booth, below us. Anachronisms fell into place. The wild country swept about us. The sun on the sea was in another world.

'It's a basalt sarcophagus. One of the grandest places I know,' said Miss Toklas, 'and the saddest.'

We sat in a cleft of the willows, out of the noon sun, on the banks of the Rhone.

'How much time out for digestion?' said Miss Stein.

'Well, not more than ten minutes,' answered Miss Toklas.

'Then, I'll tell this young man a story about St. Maximin. We can't get there. It's too far, beyond Aix. But the earliest and finest basilica is there. Romanesque, almost Roman. In the crypt was buried Mary Magdalene after a stormy voyage in middle life and an austere old age in a cell on the Sainte Baume, nearby. Of course, every one knew she was a saint; but she came up to scratch, too. Her bones worked miracles. And she was very lucrative. In the next century, the Saracens got obstreperous; and Christendom thought that St. Maximin was too near the sea to be a safe place for such pious relics. So the Pope ordered that she be sent to Vezeley, in Burgundy. The Abbot of St. Maximin was mighty unwilling to part with his treasure. He was sad when he sent off the coffin in an ark with chanting monks, a strong guard, and dozens of mules. You can just see what a fine, sweaty procession it made.

Two or three hundred years later, when the Saracens were no longer a menace, the Pope ordered the return of Mary Magdalene. Quite as the first Abbot had feared, Vezeley refused to give back so sainted, so profitable a corpse. The pilgrimage to Vezeley was famous, and St. Maximin fallen into desuetude. The Pope thundered. Vezeley backed down sufficiently to haggle. Vezeley decided to open the coffin, just for a look-see, or perhaps with an eye to the best piece. The lid was pried up. The coffin was filled with bricks: Clever old St. Maximin!'

'And then, what did they do?' I asked delighted.

'Well, then, the Pope made a compromise. Half of her was to go to Vezeley (as soon as they'd found her wherever she was secreted in the floor of her original tomb) to make up for the centuries of pious fraud. . . .'

'Bricks without straw?' suggested Miss Toklas.

'And half was to stay in St. Maximin where she belonged. And that's the way you see her today if you peek through the glass wass-ist-das, either as Vezeley or at St. Maximin.'

'Now,' said Miss Toklas, 'do help me pick up the lunch things; and you, Barlow, for God's sake, see if you can crank Lizzy. We must get on.'

'What do you say if we skip Arles?' asked Miss Stein, once we were under way. 'He's seen a better amphitheater at Nimes. And St. Trophimes is Christian and early Romanesque and not in our period today. He'll have to come back and see it. I know Arles is the pearl of the prairie, – but it can't be helped.'

'Anyhow,' Miss Toklas comforted me, 'the Roman theater isn't nearly as good as the one at Orange. All mucked up by the Saracens with watch-towers.'

We climbed into the Ford.

'Where to?' I asked, feeling a bit cheated.

'Les Baux,' said Miss Stein, and fished for the gear-shift.

'You see,' said Miss Toklas, 'we must be to Avignon before dark. We've no headlights.'

We crossed the Rhone on the bridge between Beaucaire and Tarascon.

'Unless my memory's gone haywire, the most notable Lord of Beaucaire was Aucassin,' said Miss Stein.

'Nicolete's boyfriend?' I asked carefully.

'The same.'

'Ah!' I breathed.

'Meaning what? Such a pregnant "AH!"' Miss Stein looked worried.

'Well,' I said, fathering courage. 'I remember the story. Half prose, half verse. Personally, I prefer the ballad of young Beichan who was put in a mafsymore and finally set free by Susy Pye, the daughter of the cruel Moor. Some sort of story,' I added carelessly.

'I think you made it up. Where did you get it from?'

'O, it's true enough. I read it in college.'

'But "mafsymore" . . . ?'

'Scots for dungeon.'

'No one could make that up.'

'And of course,' added Miss Toklas, 'anybody'd remember a mafsymore all his life.'

'But it is a pity,' Miss Stein concluded balefully, 'that he knows anything. A virgin page is such fun.'

I bowed from my soap-box. 'It was such an opportunity to get in my one nugget.'

'You're forgiven,' said Miss Stein, as we swung off the bridge, to rattle into the main street.

Somewhere down its course, Miss Stein began to blow the horn with unexpected vigor. I peered out. More than a block ahead of us, I saw a schoolgirl riding a bicycle, coming our way, and on our side of the road. She was going at a good clip and calling to friends over her shoulder. Blow as Miss Stein might, nothing could distract the speeding bicyclist. Miss Stein came to a full stop. On raced the schoolgirl, her hair flying, her head over her shoulder, calling to her friends on the sidewalk. The end was abrupt. The bicycle hit us squarely head on. The rider, after a graceful parabola on schoolbooks, girl, and petticoats, landed astride on the hood of the engine, face to face with Miss Stein and Miss Toklas. For one wild second she gazed through our windshield at us, and then burst into a fireworks of hysteria. Several passersby who had watched the performance from start to finish came up, assuring all concerned that we had behaved according to code and that the girl was entirely at fault. Between sobs she admitted that no bones were broken.

'Come on,' said Miss Toklas, 'let's get out of this.'

With expressions like those at the end of a letter in French, we rolled carefully out of the crowd and on our way, before the police or an irate parent could stop us.

'We're well out of that,' said Miss Stein. 'Damages are easier to collect than rent.'

We cut out of Tarascon and headed across the Crau.

Ave Dione: A Tribute

Imagine a great plain, its surface covered with round, smooth stones, about the size of cantaloupe. The north side bounded by grey-white crags, more than hills, little jagged mountains. Nothing will grow on it. Its complete isolation was perfect for a powder factory and magazine. Just about this time (1917–1918), the powder-magazine blew up. But there were no traces of disaster on the nubbly, stony, face of the crau when we passed. Judgement Day alone will disturb its arid surface. A surface which has so puzzled mankind that the ancients decided something quite out of the ordinary alone could account for it. In fact, Jupiter had hurled the stones, in profuse inaccuracy, when he dropped down to help Hercules in a fight. (Strabo is not very explicit, but it will do, as far as I'm concerned.)

We crossed, and entered the foot-hills. If Arizona were chalky, this was Arizona. 'Bad-lands,' on the sign posts, was 'Val d'Enfer.' We climbed up and up this fantastic roller-coaster. In the cupped valleys, trees and vines took root and a house or two. Then another climb between the chalk-cliffs, – like the tour of a mouse at a pastry-cooks. Always ahead and up was that last pinnacle of rock where cave-men had dug in for security and, ages later, the flower of the Renaissance had blossomed, to be blasted all too soon by Richelieu. At last we rounded a peak and almost bumped into the stone jambs of the carved gate of the town. A hundred feet more, and we had to leave the car in front of the inn; vehicles went no further. (All this was years before the English woman was murdered here by her meridional lover and chauffeur; but we probably passed her as she sat painting watercolors, as elderly English women should, and collecting the relics which had brought her to Les Baux.)

On all sides the sky slipped down, to rest southward on the bony plain of the Crau, northward on lower peaks. And on the flattened top of rock where we stood lay something broken; the splinters of a Court of Love.

73

'The first time you come to Les Baux,' said Miss Stein, 'you're struck all of a heap with wonder. The second time you come to show a friend, and you wonder there is so little really to wonder at and so little to show. And the third time, and for keeps, you know there is more here between the lines, in the sound of the place, in that window left staring on the plain after the house has gone, like a live eye in a dead hand, than almost anywhere else you can think of. Perhaps Agra is like that, but I've never been there.'

'I suppose there's no room nowadays for the kind of lyric perfection that this was in its prime,' said Miss Toklas. 'The modern equivalent is Carmel, California, or any other art colony with hot-dog stands. But in those days when they wanted a harmonious town for one purpose they built it at one sweep; and you get Les Baux and the Place Stanislas at Nancy and the Certosa at Pavia, which is almost big enough to be a town.'

'Look at this bit, and the stone-joining,' cried Miss Stein, 'put together neatly like a good page of verse or prose, without mortar visible or paddings, – just the wanted surface.'

Half the front of the house had fallen in, but on the remaining facade hung a sculptured balcony and double renaissance window. Within we could see a great chimney-piece, and carved corbels, – and everywhere a perfect workmanship. Battlements overturned, roofs fallen, but at every step some stretch of wall or some doorway or cistern or stair which cried, as the leprous wrecks cry in the Orient, for the alms of appreciation. Not one ruined inch without an electric charge of style and design.

'It's like a white Pompeii,' I said.

'Only here the devastation is more complete, because man did it. Nature is kinder,' said Miss Stein, 'after all.'

Les Baux was the last wreck. Everything else we saw that day, – in the way of double-starred sights, – was as contemporary as cheese, as standards, as timeless. Nature and man had neither blasted nor nibbled; and you could bury a general still under the monument. At St. Remy, you could pipe water over the arches on the Gard, and you can see this minute a copy of Avignon on the East River, New York City, in the new and towering Hospital.

The long pull from Les Baux to the Gard took us through a country that had so much character of its own that it recalled every other place on earth. Yet, of course, the resemblance runs the other way. The children resemble the Mother. Other places, bits of other scenes, look like this, but this looks like itself, eternally. It has so much character that it frightens some people. And, in spite of the sun and the color, it is austere.

First we ran down the chalk cliffs again, – another way from the way we had come. Right through the bleached gorges till the hills broke down into rolling country and the softer cultivation of the Rhone Valley. Where tramping legions first felt the downward slant under their feet and saw below them the rich green and the white cities, lies St. Remy: and there a Roman general erected an arch after some forgotten triumph and raised a tomb for some forgotten hero, – probably himself.

We drew up by the side of the road and got out. We walked under the arch, counting how many men abreast could have marched through; we circled the tomb, to wonder at the clean edges of the frieze, the energy of the life-size figures, the not quite metropolitan air, like that of any proper frontier monument.

'A mousetrap is a mousetrap,' said Miss Stein, 'but it catches queer fish. I remember how George Moore set a trap out in his Dublin yard because he was sure the hungry cat, belonging to his neighbors, the Misses Drew, had designs on his own pet blackbird. And one day the trap clicked. And what do you suppose it caught? The blackbird, of course. Now here's a general who thought he was celebrating an immortal triumph. And what has he caught? An unexpected afterglow.

The real triumph is that nearly two thousand years later you and I should make a pilgrimage to this spot. Really far more of a compliment than the shouts of his soldiers, who were pretty well paid.'

We sat on a low stone parapet to watch the sunset, over the hills of the far side of the valley, turn all our shadows to purple and burnish every westward surface.

'It looks just as it must have looked then,' said Miss Toklas. 'This pine grove must be the child of the one growing then. Not a house in sight. Perhaps that's what makes this arch and this tomb more endearing than the usual heavily-starred gasp-producers. The Via Appia and the Forum are too decayed, and the others always have a lying-in hospital or something built next door.'

'And it seems to me,' I said, 'that I've seen plenty of copies of these two. All our architects have had a long, lingering, but not last, look. The coffered ceiling under the arch is an old friend, Gor blimey!'

'Come on,' said Miss Stein to Miss Toklas, 'and let's get into the car before we find out that he knows something and spoils it all.'

'And it's miles to Remouline! If the sun's on time today, we'll only just make it.'

As we ran across the plain in that last one golden hour of day that in the south lasts two, Miss Toklas turned and imparted information.

'The Pont du Gard is not the least because it is the most lonely. Perhaps it's the best thing we shall have seen today, because, precisely, it has no background. I mean that with a temple or a tomb precisely, it has no background. I mean that with a temple or a tomb or a robber-baron's castle there are a thousand connotations to help us; and, if we like to imagine the legionnaires or ladies in wimples, we enjoy the sight of what remains of those days. But at the Pont du Gard there are no accessories, and there never were any. It is an aqueduct, as utilitarian as the Brooklyn Bridge. If it seems good to us now, it's because it just is good. Just as the Brooklyn Bridge is good and always will be, partly accidentally; a thing perfectly adapted to its material and its performance. And because of the scale it's on, it is unbelievably noble. You'll see. In this dusk it will be some lovely color, like everything that's made of stone: but the color is unimportant, and sentimental of us. The line, the mass, – the things Rodin and Maillol talk about – are there.'

At Remoulins we turned up the valley of the Gard and wound with the stream through foothills, getting ever higher. The Gard rushed past us, gurgling, with trout and pebbles in its throat. Presently the hills became steeper, shutting the stream into a small canyon that turned and twisted so that we could not see ahead. Then, suddenly, we came to a straight stretch; across the gorge, at the far end, rose the bridge, from great arches anchored in the stream, then from tier on tier of smaller ones, – like a quickening tempo, to the level top, flush with the sky and the table-lands on either side.

It had a rhythm that beat out at us, and a vibration like the sound of trumpets.

The three of us sat stunned by such magnificence. For myself, I felt that all tourism and curiosity was a cheap thing. I felt the asymmetry of most of our lives was a patent affront to this aqueduct; before it a man could not be trivial unwittingly.

Our talk was subdued. The night air was chilly. We were half way along the road to Avignon before our conversation reverted to the blytheness which had sustained it all day. Miss Stein recovered first.

'It is pleasant to think that the Pont du Gard was built to carry fresh water to the baths in Nimes,' she said. 'It is more curious and un- pleasant to realize that for centuries Christianity was the only religion which almost made an official dogma of dirt. I think the Church has always mishandled two things, water and gunpowder, making them useful instead of decorative. It used one to drink and the other to blow up the people. The Chinese made fireworks and the pagans built the Pont du Gard, bless 'em.'

It was night when we reached Avignon. The Ford possessed parking lamps which just kept us within the law.

As we reached the Rhone, with the white city, – its lights atwinkle – across the river, Miss Stein pulled to the side, at the bridgehead.

'A first look from here; you'll never forget it. Just climb down the bank a yard or two,' she said.

I scrambled down till the Rhone eddied at my feet. A hundred yards to my left, the Pont d'Avignon thrust its shorn span into the water. '*Sur le pont d'Avignon . . .*' my mother's voice came back to me. My own childhood; the childhood of France, too, when people of that lovely twelfth century could believe that Little Benny, the wandering Monk, had built the bridge miraculously overnight; back to the childhood of Europe, when the boatmen, poling up the river, shouted, 'Ave, Dione!' as they passed the bluff where the Goddess's temple gleamed, and where now, opposite me, I saw the white line of the battlements rise to make the great facade of the Palace of the Popes.

I returned to the car.

'You told me nothing,' I said. 'It is the most beautiful city in the world.' I felt the choke in my throat that perfect romantic beauty brings, – not sad, not sentimental at all, I like to believe. I always got it half way through the Overture to Meistersinger, and think no less of myself for it.

'You will come back many times,' said Miss Toklas, 'and when you're not here you'll dream about it.'

'I don't want to dream,' I said. 'I want to think about it, all awake. I want to be able always to recall every inch of our day, every moment, every shape, every color, – everything you said!' (I was, after all, very young, very hopeful, and very much impressed.)

'God forbid!' said Miss Stein.

Ave Dione: A Tribute

After thirty odd years, quotation marks are hazards. But if I have misquoted Miss Stein, I have not misquoted my wonder, my indebtedness, which hung on her words. If I have let her gaiety down, it's that I'm not as witty as she. Perhaps on her profound simplicity I have hung the banners of my youthful exuberance. But the homage is there: in thirty years of travel, each journey has found me turning off to make a pilgrimage to a shrine which she set up in my heart. If I have foisted any subsequent book-learning upon our so-spontaneous day, that too is a tribute to her. For I had, over the years, to live up to her Provence by learning about it. She would like that. She would be thrilled if anyone read this, packed bags at once, and set out for the valley of the Rhone, to the old Ligurian cities, to the bridge across which the Lord of Beaucaire looked down and Le Roi Rene looked up. (History records that it was a dirty look.) To Tarascon, the golden, which has never recovered from Daudet's awful gift: Tartarin. To Avignon, where those with long memories cried, 'Ave Dione.'

ROBERT MCALMON

Robert McAlmon, born in Kansas City, was a poet, novelist, publisher, and editor who joined the U.S. avant-garde literary movement in New York when he established and co-edited the journal *Contact* with William Carlos Williams. Transplanted to Paris in the 1920s, the journal evolved into a publishing house whose authors included Hemingway, Hilda Doolittle, Ezra Pound, Dorothy Richardson, and Winifred Bryher (then McAlmon's wife). In 1923, Contact Editions published 505 copies of Stein's *The Making of Americans*. McAlmon also published his own books, including the short story collection *A Hasty Bunch* and the novel *Post-Adolescence*.

When Gertrude Stein first met McAlmon, she thought he was 'very mature and very good-looking.' But he was also egotistical and independent, and inevitably they quarreled. He lost interest in Stein's writings, for reasons he explains in this excerpt from his memoir, *Being Geniuses Together*. For her part, Stein concluded that although he was a prolific writer, much of what he wrote was dull.

from *Being Geniuses Together*

PORTRAIT

Gertrude Stein being a Sumerian monument at five o'clock tea on Fleurus Street among Picassos, Braques, and some Cézannes; slowly the slow blush monumentally mounting as in dismay pontificating Miss Stein loses herself in the labyrinthine undergrowths of her jungle-muddy forestial mind naïvely intellectualizing.

Early 1925, speaking of herself, Miss Stein said, 'No, nobody has done anything to develop the English language since Shakespeare, except myself, and Henry James perhaps a little.'

'Yes, the Jews have produced only three originative geniuses: Christ, Spinoza, and myself.'

Miss Stein has been disconcerted by her thick intuitions having slowly suspected that her oracular proclamations are being adjudged rather than accepted as mediumistic deliverances of nature's slow-aged, giving-taking, uninterruptable continuance.

Slowly the slow blush mounts and her tone is of naïve plaint; embarrassment struggling suspiciously to exasperation. 'But my manner could not remind you of anything Sumerian. I have never gone in for Babylonian writings.'

Being, biblical, being obsessed with being, biblical, repetitively

Excerpt from *Being Geniuses Together,* by Robert McAlmon (New York: Doubleday, 1968), 227–31. Reprinted by permission of the author and the Watkins/Loomis Agency.

being, biblical, massively being, the slow slime breathes to being, slowly the biblical slime evolves to being. The aged elephant mastadonically heaves to being, breathing in the slow slime with aged hope, breathing to be slowly. Slowly burdened with a slowly massive clinging slime, agedly the slow elephant ponderously moves in the ancient slime, slowly breathing to move heaving the idea, being; disconcertedly the slow blush mounts and the infant elephant idea panics at being adjudged rather than consulted as an oracle; the ancient mastodonic slow idea with slow suspicion moves agedly suspectful, resting to pause in the ancient slime, effortfully feeling slow being, going on being, to be evolving towards the slowly massive idea elephant, while slowly the elephantine idea evolves to the idea slow aged elephant, suspiciously being, heaving from the slime.

'She is shy, very unsure of herself,' the mind warns a listener. 'Don't frighten her or she won't talk and when she talks one can, if keen, select an idea which may be heavy but which may also be unique. The elephant's sensibility is not that of the humming bird's.'

Shyly pleased by 'Of course, you are not touched by time, so you need not think of your generation. Even the youngsters have not the sense of modernity which you had before the war,' Miss Stein is monumentally deaf to the tones of flattery or irony. She confesses confidingly, naïvely being naïve.

'I sometimes wonder how anybody can read my work when I look it over after a time. It seems quite meaningless to me at times. Of course, when I write it it seems luminous and fine and living, and as you say it has a tremendous pulsation.'

The slow earth moves agedly, massively the mastodon stirs in the mind, and slimed with mud is mud, pulsating with and in mud, but ponderously this mud slowly evolves to the identity, slowly to ponderously identify itself as an idea, slowly evolved, slowly dredged through the snow clinging mud, slowly to capture the slow slimed identity of the aged slow idea, elephant.

Leo Stein has said, from 1917 on: 'Gertrude does not know what words mean. She hasn't much intuition but thickly she has sensations, and of course her mania, herself. Her idea of herself as a genius.'

Leo Stein has said often: 'Gertrude write a thesis against pragmatism which would win William James' admiration? She couldn't. Gertrude can't think consecutively for ten seconds. It was only after I discovered Picassos and had them in the studio for two years that Gertrude began to think she senses a quality.'

Gertrude, in speaking of her work. 'No, oh no, no, no, no, that isn't possible. You would not find a painter destroying any of his sketches. A writer's writing is too much of the writer's being; his flesh child. No, no, I never destroy a sentence or a word of what I write. You may, but of course, writing is not your métier, Doctor.'

The Doctor-writer: 'But Doctor Stein, you are sure that writing is your métier? I solve the economies of life through the profession of doctoring, but from the first my will was towards writing. I hope it pleases you, but things that children write have seemed to me so Gertrude Steinish in their repetitions. Your quality is that of being slowly and innocently first recognizing sensations and experience.'

'I could not see him after that,' Miss Stein said later. 'I told the maid I was not in if he came again. There is too much bombast in him.'

Slowly moving towards a slow idea the slow child repeating the idea being, slowly the child entangles itself in slow bewilderment of the forest of slow ideas; slowly the shy slow blush slowly mounts in suspicion slowly tormented by the harassing distrust, an idea, slowly but finally lost, slowly rediscovered, slowly emerging, slowly escaping, slowly confusion gathers, the dark blush mounts, while slow panic reveals that surely Miss Stein has slowly entangled herself and has slowly allowed the slow idea she was slowly expounding to slowly escape and slowly lost in slow confusion of slow panic shyly slowly Miss Stein wishes these people who listen adjudgingly rather than as to an oracle were away, slowly she is ill at ease, and slowly she realizes suddenly that she wishes these people quickly away, and quickly they go, slowly controlling themselves to quickly realize laughter upon relentlessly realizing being, surely, being outside, away from Miss Stein.

Back in Paris there was a period which was very Einstein or relativist. J. W. N. Sullivan arrived from London and lingered about the Quarter. He was interested in music, as befits a higher mathematician, and he was still passionate about Dostoevsky, who had been the inspiration for Einstein's discoveries. One day he and I called on Ezra, and somehow whenever Sullivan was about there was profound discussion, whether he was with Eliot, Pound, Wyndham Lewis, or myself. Ezra assured Sullivan that he highly overrated Dostoevsky, for Ezra was inclined to grant 'them Rooshians' very short shrift indeed. Sullivan and I must have had the same bright suspicion at the same moment, because simultaneously we insisted that Ezra say which book of Dostoevsky's and of what Russian writers he was speaking. Ezra backed down gracefully, for his knowledge of Russian literature from the actual reading of it was very slight. Years before he had made the statement in print that one need not have read a book or an author to have a fairly clear idea about a book's quality, so neither Sullivan nor I pressed our victory.

Today I wonder if time will prove Einstein to have made such valuable discoveries as everybody so aggressively claimed in those days? Reading Munthe's *San Michele* and his account of the hypnotist converts, one may wonder what a later generation will think of psychoanalysts and Einstein. I found, however, that I like these higher mathematicians. They have an innocence and a limpid quality of sweet expectancy and gentleness which is appealing. Evidently, from Gertrude Stein's account, Whitehead had these qualities of tender concern about human destiny also. Possibly higher mathematics is the final romanticism after all.

PAVEL TCHELITCHEW

Like many Russian aristocrats, the family of Pavel Tchelitchew fled from its home during the Bolshevik Revolution. In 1918 Tchelitchew found himself in Kiev, where he studied drawing at the Kiev Academy. His flight continued, taking him to Turkey, to Berlin, and then to Paris in 1923. Much of his work was as a scenic designer for theater and ballet, including sets for Diaghilev's startling new company. His painting suggests inspiration from Picasso's ascetic Harlequins, which Tchelitchew stretched and distorted even further. Throughout his work, in the pained figures, shattered faces, and somber tones, there is evidence of his own suffering and torments. 'Strindberg was said to have been possessed by a dark demon,' Harold Acton commented, 'but [Tchelitchew] must have been possessed by several.'

The atmosphere in his Rue Jacques Mawas studio was fittingly macabre. There, Acton observed, the artist would spend his days moping in the company of his 'stolid Russian sister and a Frenchified American friend who sat thumping the piano in his dressing gown.' When he was able to paint, he devoted much of his creative energy to experimentation. 'Though [Tchelitchew] pretended to have a horror of fashion,' Acton again noted, 'he could not help courting it.' And fellow artist Francis Rose concurred, adding, 'He was always searching and twisting in different directions, as if he were afraid of dropping behind the times.' For a time he painted with a mixture of coffee grounds, sand, and gouache.

Pavel Tchelitchew, Portrait of Gertrude Stein, brush with black ink on ivory wove paper (1930). Gift of Mrs. Gilbert W. Chapman in memory of Charles B. Goodspeed. Photograph courtesy The Art Institute of Chicago.

Although Gertrude Stein was pleased with his portrait of her, Acton felt an intense dislike for the bald, elongated head and clotted forehead that Tchelitchew painted as his likeness. Like the portrait of Dorian Gray, it was, Acton feared, what he might become.

If Acton's response was less than enthusiastic, it was more than compensated by the support of Edith Sitwell. Gertrude Stein introduced the painter to the poet and she quickly became one of his favorite subjects. Dame Edith dedicated two poems to him, sat for six portraits and a sculpture in wax on wire, and described him as 'that tragic, haunted, and noble artist – one of the most generous human beings I have even known.'

Although Tchelitchew was successful as an artist in France, he was never able to consider it his home. He felt intensely foreign, he admitted in a letter to Gertrude Stein. He considered himself 'a Russian Negro among the French.'

Before World War II, Tchelitchew left Paris and immigrated to the United States. In his New York studio he began a satirical surrealistic painting, *Phenomena,* which showed, among other things, Gertrude Stein squatting on a heap of broken canvas. Tchelitchew died in 1957.

Editor's note: This selection is a transcription of a lecture delivered by Tchelitchew at Yale University. Errors in syntax and grammar reflect Tchelitchew's level of proficiency in English. Occasionally, I have added words in brackets to help the reader make sense of particular passages. Words that are unclear in the transcription are indicated by [?] in the text. In a few places, I have eliminated a word or two, replaced by ellipses, to keep the sense of a sentence.

Martin A. Ryerson Lecture, February 20, 1951

in connection with the Gertrude Stein exhibition

Ladies and Gentlemen:

I am very pleased to come to talk to you about Gertrude Stein. She was my great friend, in fact I owe her everything that happened to me since the time I met her. Because from a very obscure person I suddenly became a young artist on whom there was put a spot of light. I agreed to come to talk to you first because in general I don't like when artists speak about art, except in private gatherings to each other, friends, or poets or musicians, when it's all very private, it's never public. Everything what I heard public when artists spoke about art, that was rather disastrous. For speaking about art, there are scholars on art, like that, for speaking about literature and poetry, there are scholars in the same field. Well, Gertrude Stein has given you her manuscripts, her letters. I in my humble way have given you my sketchbooks. My sketchbooks are my thoughts. There you can see where my mind was wandering and why. And later on maybe it will be interesting and maybe it will inspire somebody. Besides young people, there are always young minds interested in Gertrude Stein. She was extremely interested in what the younger generation had to think, what they had to say, what they were going to do, what is the future development of that strange mechanism called the human mind. You

From the Gertrude Stein Collection, Yale Collection of American Literature, Beinecke Rare Book and Manuscript Library, Yale University. Published by permission of the Yale University Library.

know about Bruisy [Brewsie] and Willie, et cetera. I inherited from her great interest in young minds and I decided that I am going to talk to you, that I am going to talk to you about Gertrude Stein as a poet, as she revealed herself being poet in talks, in conversations, in certain attitudes, in certain remarks, and what I thought she was meaning when she was saying this, in reply to when I was saying that, et cetera. My friend, Mr. Virgil Thomson, the great composer, who composed her 'The Mother of Us All' and 'Four Saints in Three Acts' will come here and talk to you. Poetry and music have very much in common. He was her close friend, until the last days, and collaborator. So he will tell you all about music, the relations of music and her poetry. I will speak about my ideas what her poetry was. I hope it will not sound very pretentious. But I have my points which I hope I will prove you what I would like to say. Gertrude Stein is a great genius, a great person, and it is a vast subject, and there can't be one point, there are many points of view on that subject, and many points of view maybe one day will culminate in really seeing what it all was. It is too new, (we think) there is too much that is a little obscure, incomprehensible, so let's see what I have to say to you.

Will you excuse me for my English which is not very clear, which has accent. I speak several languages, they all have accents. I can't help it. I'll tell you why. Because artists, we do not think with words. We work with forms, not with words. Musicians work with sounds, also not with words. So you forgive me about that, please. And besides, I must tell you that I have to speak sometimes about myself, and you forgive me that, too because *I* saw her, *I* talked to her, and not to somebody else. And I don't want you to ask me any questions. My pet hate is questions and you understand why, because I come here as a friend. And it's all about my private life, about our relations and friendship, and it is not at all a subject of public discussion. I'll tell to you what I want to tell, and I will not tell you what I don't want to tell. So would Gertrude Stein, you will not get out of her anything what she wouldn't like to tell you. There is an enigma in every relation, and in every friendship, and in every reverence. But whatever I have to say I hope it will be not obscure, and it will be not puzzling or confusing, because . . . I will tell you and reply [to] you with some words by your writer, Thoreau, who said, 'do not suppose I have a taint of obscurity.' I will speak about Gertrude Stein as a poet, great, famous, and courageous person – figure. Well, speaking about poetry, it is very difficult to say. Where is the climate of poetry? Where is it that poetry originates? It is very difficult to explain to you. You know very well it starts from the forgotten past of the magic ritual. In the words of the high priest, the words that contained life and death, fear and happiness. As it says in the fairytales about the Firebird, it's beyond the Seven Seas. At the end of the night – at the end of the night there is the garden of Hesperides. And there grow the trees, the apple trees, of eternity. And the Firebird, swift as the lightning, Firebird of inspiration, flies there. If you catch his feather he'll give you the apples of eternity. You see, it's all very far and it's all very strange and what I have to say seems to you probably strange. I am like an old folklore storyteller. So, I will try to explain [to] you my point of view about this very strange, unusual thing – what is poetical inspiration – because the sources of poetical inspiration are equal for us, and for composers, and for poets. And I hope I will be not confusing, and I hope I will not confuse you more than you are, and I could prove to some when they say about me that I am confused, it is not me who's confused – they simply don't understand. And also I would like to prove to Miss Alice B. Toklas, the faithful companion of Gertrude Stein, that painters not only paint but also can think sometimes. Well, here we are.

I came to Paris in 1923 in July. I was urged to come to Paris by Serge Paul (Pavlik) Diaghilev, the great magician of the Russian ballet. You know all about ballet, you know all about it, I have nothing to talk to you. But I came too late for the ballet to do anything. I had been making ballets in Berlin, I had to do an opera for Staatsoper, I was very busy and I had no knowledge that the season in Paris is June and July, and after the fourteenth of July, after les Grands-eaux de Versailles, everything is closed, Paris is dead, everybody except cats, dogs, and concierges are gone and there is nobody there. Well, but I arrived in Paris with American friends. I had made lots of friends in Berlin, and I suppose that's why I am now American, too. There was my friend, the pianist, Allen Tanner, and George Antheil, your composer. The day we arrived we knew from a friend that there was a great event in the Theatre Michel. In the Theatre Michel was a per- formance of a poetical – might we say – drama, or what it was by Tristan Tzara called 'Le Coeur à Gaz,' ('Gas Lit Heart'), but besides that we were warned that there would be an event of a most Parisian kind. There was a schism between Dada and Surrealist, and there will be *abagarre,* that means fight, a performance, not only on the stage but in the public. I didn't like that kind of thing very much because [of] lots of it in my young days. I was then twenty-five and most of you probably hadn't been born. So it was all like Marco Polo and his China. Well, we went there. We came to the theater very early, it was all filled . . . and the moment the performance started we heard something unusual pervading the audience. Finally, whistles, screams, awful words, you know the kind of words – they were not printing that sort of words in my time but now I suppose they're printing them now. So, start everything, scream and yell, vociferate, and men were run- ning on stage, and men were running from the audience, and ladies with rather disheveled coiffeurs were screaming awful words, too, and finally we couldn't hear anything at all. I saw a young man with blond hair, blue eyes, and top hat, and morning coat with pink cheeks like two apples, screaming and yelling, *'Mon baline est blanc d'Espagne, je me tue Madeleine, Madeleine'* and then he received something in his figure and that was my friend, René Crevel. And I say to my friend, 'Let's get out of here.' He say, 'No, no, no, we have to see.' Finally arrived the police and everything, and everything nicely settled down. Well, I left the theater. I didn't know anything about the play, and I thought the boys behaved very much like the school boys and didn't please me very much. I had a very poor opinion about French poets, I must confess [to] you. So I would like to speak to you about Paris of those days.

Paris is a very beautiful town. It's all pale grey. All in gardens. Chestnut trees blooming and all this is all very extraordinary aspect for somebody at a very ugly town like Berlin. Diaghilev told me, 'You cannot stay in the provinces, it's just not possible. You have to come to Paris.' So, Paris was beautiful, but I found myself not very well at ease. Through some friends of Diaghilev I met other friends, and I knew some of the great men of that time. I saw them at dinners, I saw them at the tea parties, I saw Paul Valéry, I saw others, Bergson was the great god of that time. And the poets' leading figure was Anna de Noailles, poetess. She was a woman of certain age, she was sometimes, I remember her photographs when I was a young boy, in her elegant dresses in the fashion papers with big eyes and fringe and hobble skirts. You see it was a long time ago. But I saw her already a very tired figure. Her face was covered with powder, like with dust, her eyes were covered with ashes, that was makeup up to her ears. She had rather bright colored dresses, lace and fringes, and gold embroideries. Lots of jewelry, tulles, and one really couldn't believe that a person like that could be a poet. I knew her poetry, it was very charming. Well, she would come to dinner, eat enormously – those dinner parties were ordeals because you were sitting between two ladies who were chatting all the time. Chatter unending. Food endless. You couldn't eat because by the time one [stopped] . . . talking to you the other one would start talking to you. They would not give you time to reply, or to breathe, or to swallow, because they would have everything to say. To laugh, to tell you everything not listening to you, to make you frightful eyes, to smile, to laugh again, to turn their back to you to talk to their neighbor, to say anything, then turn back to you, and so it was until the end of dinner. It was very long. And then after that Madame Noailles would get up – and before she would arrive to the dinner because the young men were supposed to come very early, earlier than others, young men like the flowers in Paris salons they have to be early, they have to be there to be surrounding the hostess, they are the human flowers. So, all the men would arrive, would arrive, rush immediately to the books of the poetess and find some lines to say, and the moment the dinner is over they rush to her, kneel around her couch, – she was like Madame Récamier – and all those old ambassadors, and lawyers, and businessmen would sit there like pet dogs and speak, 'Oh, this is divine. Oh, this line is splendid.' I knew that they hadn't looked at the book. So, then she would start, very tired, because she had an enormous appetite. She would lie down there and speak about love, and that was the time for me, I have to run away. And in spite of what my hostess would think, I say, 'No, no, no I have to paint, I *have* to paint,' and I would rush out and walk in Paris, walk in the Bois de Boulogne, walk in the avenue du Bois, and go up to Montparnasse, and it would take me a long time. And I would see the life, early morning light begin, and I see the *tombereau,* the carriages with cabbages and with carrots, and the healthy people and the real life arriving, after I had seen that burlesque with this literary salon. There were serious literary salons, naturally, besides that, like that the Duchesse de Rochefoucauld, et cetera, but I was fed up with these salons for my first year in Paris, and I decided I would not go any more, and I would not lose my time, and I would not see poets.

Well, I met in Paris a very extraordinary person, Miss Jane Heap and Miss Margaret Anderson; they were both editing *The Little Review.* They were very courageous persons. They published Gertrude Stein the first time. They published James Joyce. James Joyce was judged obscene and then they went to jail. And there was a trial. But you mustn't be surprised that James Joyce was found obscene. They found Brancusi obscene. Well, you know you can see how points of view have changed. I heard about Gertrude Stein and about Alice Toklas from

Jane Heap, and after two years being in Paris I met them. I had an exhibition, I sent two pictures at the Salon d'Automne, that is the annual exhibition where you have to do it at least once in your lifetime. It is sort of an official appearance, like a debut, so I have to make that debut, too. And I have my great friend, the cubist painter, Marcoussis, who promised me he would give me a decent wall so I was not lost among monstrosities, because Matisse who used sometimes to be in the jury used to say, 'It is so awful if I would see my own picture and I wouldn't know that I had recommended it, I would say "Refusée" because such horrible stuff was sent there.' So, I knew Marcoussis, so I sent the picture and accepted, and there was among those pictures *The Strawberry Basket,* which you probably saw reproduced. And on the way back with Jane Heap from the vernissage on the Pont Royale just going to the Tuilleries, I saw Gertrude Stein and Alice B. Toklas. They were coming in their little car, that was, I couldn't find out really what it was because I think it was a Model T Ford. When she bought that car, after the war or during the war, that car was just stripped to the essences, it was naked, that's why the car was called, 'Lady Godiva,' because she was naked. And . . . it was so high that in spite of time, that time, the cars were very high, this car was like a mountain. It was a small mountain itself. And Gertrude Stein and Alice B. Toklas sitting in it were higher than anybody, taxis or anything that passed around. So I met her and she was very sorry that we were leaving. I must describe to you a little bit how Gertrude was dressed. Well, it's very strange. She was dressed in a way of very simple essential fashions that were not fashions of that day. There was nothing extraordinary, nothing mad, nothing exaggerated. It was the simplest bell-shaped skirt and bell-shaped coat with big pockets where she could put keys, and gloves and candy, because she loved candy, and there was candy for me sometimes later on, too. And, a very simple hat, sort of a [cap] – that you could put in your pocket – because she put the cap in there, too. Alice was dressed in great elegance, but also very simple. She used to have capes with pockets, like that, she could put her arms in; she used to have big white gloves, and hats. And the hats of Alice were extraordinary. She loved hats and I remember lots of hats of hers and one I'll never forget. It was grey-green felt, like plush, and on this felt was dozens of mustard green birds, and I used to call that hat, 'The Cemetery of Birds.' But Alice loved that cemetery very well. Gertrude used to comment on her hats that Alice had three or four kinds of hats. There's the hat of a great success. This hat can go for long years and sometimes be worn — that's a great love. The second hat was the kind good, very good, it would go for three months. Then, the hat that was all right for a few weeks. And there was a hat which was a failure. It saw half a day's time, it arrived, it was put on, and — it died that day. And so Gertrude would say, 'And so with art.'

Next day Gertrude Stein visited my studio during my absence. (I used to go sometimes drawing in the Bois de Boulogne.) She was accompanied by Jane Heap. I had a few drawings in my studio on the walls, and a few back of the chairs, and a few here and a few there, and some pictures, but most of my drawings since my childhood I keep under lock. I don't like anybody gets in my drawings and sees anything. I have several sisters, so you can understand. Women are very, very curious. I found out later that men are equally curious, so it doesn't matter. But still I always kept it under lock. So, when she knew that, she was very disappointed and she wanted to go away. But my friends who were there said, 'Why don't you open the cupboard?' So she sent my friends downstairs and out of her car they found that instrument that we call in French '*la clef anglaise*' something that you drill, drill, but anyhow that was the end of the door of my cupboard. But the fact was that she saw my drawings without me. And she was very pleased to see them and left word for me to come to see her, and I went next day and she told me how much she was interested in what I am doing. And, she thought she was very pleased that I kept under lock everything that I was doing, for she did it that way. She had two brothers, you see. So, we became great friends from that moment on. I was very pleased, because to the difference of what poets I have seen, I have also seen Monsieur [Jean] Cocteau. I was not very much pleased with what I have seen in Monsieur Cocteau, and I left it right there. I promised him a drawing, and I must confess I have never given it. I liked Gertrude Stein because there was something in her extremely friendly, extremely good, extremely maternal, and something like somebody one has always known. She was so kind and she was so thoughtful, and her appearance was so relaxing, and the things she was saying with laughter were so young. Really maternal was pleasing to me that very feminine, very kind, because I loved very much my mother. I have a great reverence for my mother and for a very great lady that I call 'Mrs. Nature.' It is sort of a name, pet name, for what is called 'The Great White Goddess.' If you have ever read [a] book by Robert Graves of that name you'll find wonderful and fascinating things there. . . . You know, now, nowadays every French young man and girl speaks English, but that time nobody spoke English. Nobody went even across the Channel. *Pourquoi?* Because France was the Rome of the Renaissance, . . . France was the leading spirit. All the rest were frankly provinces. Excuse me, for you and for my country and for everybody. Because even our great composers like Stravinsky or Prokofiev or even [Paul] Hindemith, I think they all more or less went to Paris. So, her position in France was that she was an American poet, therefore, she was respected. Nobody read her, but she was poet and that was really enough. But more than that, she was the one who discovered great French painters. She and her brothers paid their attention to Matisse in old good days when Matisse was unknown. Later on, my compatriot, Tchoutkine, was very much interested in Matisse. I saw Matisse in Russia, very, very long time ago before I came even abroad and there are very lovely Matisses there in Russia. Then Gertrude Stein discovered Picasso. And all the battle about cubism and all the scandals which you know – if you are interested there are books written, I have not read – was all attached to her name. She was the one who had believed in him. She was the one whom he painted. She was really his great friend and protector. And she was. I was extremely touched when she paid attention to me, because I was Russian and in French literary circles Russians as well as like Americans, we were in the same position. There was no easel art. You had no great painters. You had no Poussins, you had no [Antoine] Watteaus, you had no [Henri] Laurens, etcetera, alors. We had no great easel painters. We had no famous painters, there was no Russian easel art, and so I was regarded with contempt because they were French, they had great painters and great French painters still continue to be.

Well, I like to talk to you something about Russian art. I always thought it was so French that people would talk like that, because after all it took about five hundred years of great sleep of Greece between the last Byzantine chef d'oeurve and El Greco, and El Greco was never Spanish. His proportions are eleven heads in a body and those are Byzantine proportions. It is like our *fresques* [frescos] done by Greeks. Greeks came to Russia without Greek Orthodox religion; they brought art. Art was religious, art was done by monks. In the monasteries there were schools. Later on when I was in Kiev I met some of the leading monk painters and some of the pupils. Pictures were never signed. The picture was painted for glory of God, not of man. Monk artists were very much revered, and when they used to die they were elevated to sainthood. We have from the eleventh century on, we have extraordinary *fresques* and everything, frankly I think from what is seen . . . near Constantinople and what is seen in Hagia Sofia in Constantinople, and what is seen later on is seen mostly in Russia. Because the *fresques* of Russia filled the gap between the great block of Byzantine art and Cimabue. We had a great master there call St. Master Dionysios who painted church *fresques* in Novgorod and Pskof and in the wonderful church of the Savior in [?]. I think this war has done an awful damage, and I don't think they are there. Monks used to work like in companies. There was a great monk, the first, a very important artist who was responsible for all. He was the one who has to draw the whole composition. Then, he painted faces, the next one painted the clothes, the next one painted the hands, the next one painted the feet, and the next one painted the landscapes. Before they start to do that they would fast for six weeks, and the most extraordinary thing is that it looked like it was painted by the same man. The greatest honor in Russia was when a Prince or Tsar would like to give to a general or to somebody who was extremely valiant or someone who has done something very wonderful for him he will give him an icon of the saint of the name which was of the recipient's name – for Basile he would give a Saint Basile, for Peter a Saint Peter, for John a Saint John. It was so much to [protect] that painting that those icons were covered with protective covers of gold, of silver, and covered with precious stones, because they wanted to protect those paintings so much that they wouldn't be spoiled. And when now during the Revolution those protections were taken away, you could see the paint as fresh as painted yesterday. I saw myself wonderful *fresques* by our very great painter whose name was Nadrei Rublyov. He was a monk, fifteenth century, and I remember also [Sergey Pavlovich] Diaghilev when we became great friends and when he used to know what I wanted to do and saw my pictures, he used to come often to my studio. He used to tell me, 'Pavel, you are mad, you are mad. There are no Russian Tsars, but if you are succeeding doing what you are doing, then you will be after Andrei Rublyov.'

Three hundred years since Byzantine art fell asleep in Russia. Because when Peter the Great started to make changes, great changes in Russian ways, he brought from Holland frightful portraits. He didn't bring Rembrandt or he didn't bring Frans Hals. He brought third-class monstrosities. And he called the monks and ordered them to paint his portrait in that style. And all the monks refused, because they said, 'We do not paint anybody, even a Tsar, we only paint the images that belong to religion. And Tsar is not religion.' Monks were persecuted and sent to Siberia, the most frightful thing happened, but they had refused that. And since that time the Byzantine tradition and Byzantine art, and the purity and the glory of that art was falling asleep. Peter the Great had an idea. We had in Russia slaves, . . . they were peasants. So he suggested to the rich owners to send those boys, like he had gone himself, abroad to France, to Holland and to Germany to learn how to paint little paintings, and come back. So, in the eighteenth century we had that sort of art. There were some handsome portraits that will really survive, because the private, very well-known painter of the nineteenth century, Kiprensky, was flogged because he painted his landlady and she didn't have straight eyes and he wanted it her to resemble. Later on he was liberated and he became a great painter.

When I was living in Russia I was frightfully annoyed with all of that. Because at my time, in our surroundings of painter[s], art had really only one French great promising artist, that name of artist is Christian Bérard. You've all heard about Christian Bérard. He was an extraordinary young man with amazing gifts. He really had golden hands. I was so annoyed about all this picking on foreigners in Paris that I called Paris because of so many foreigners – lots of my Russian friends, there were Chinese, there were Japanese, there were most of all Spaniards, et cetera – I told them that it was Rome in the time of the barbarians. And they have never forgiven me that.

As you know Gertrude Stein was a pupil of William James. She worked under him in an insane asylum, among [aggravated?] people. Her great interest was in the functioning of a human brain – reaction. She was very much interested in how the ideas originate. Where the art starts? There we were back again at the end of the night. What is the symbolical meaning of art as revealed through an object? She practiced automatic writing. You know what automatic writing is? I practiced automatic drawing often in the forties. I have drawn lots and lots of it in my life, because in the first years when I knew Gertrude Stein she told me she didn't think I'd do well. And I did thousands of drawings since. You see, I did owe her that, too. She wanted to know through the automatic writing the language of our psyche. We don't think of anything, we concentrate on something like we're making doodles that become something. You see something in the doodles so you write words that become words, become something. She knew that her poetry was originated in a magic of the bygone days. You know very well that we can speak about poetry only since Orpheus. We have very little remnants of the Egyptian poetry, and lots of things are not deciphered. But, anyhow, we know Greek poetry. All what we have inherited in Western art came from Greece, originated in Egypt, then it came to Greece, from Greece to Italy, from Italy to France, and now here. Orpheus's name is Egyptian and Phoenician. It is composed out of two words – *aur* (light), and *rophoe* (cheering health). He got his name from his profession. He was a physician, by means of light, enlightenment. Eurydice, 'Euridike' in Greece, also Phoenician. It has come from two words – *rohe* (vision, clarity, evidence), and *dich* (that which teaches or shows), *eu* (that which is good, happy or perfect in its kind). I quote it all from Fabre d'Olivet's commentaries on the Golden Verses of Pythagoras, a most wonderful book. (I don't know if it's translated.) Art is revealed life or psyche, through sounds, words, or forms. It is revealed in order, in certain patterns, in certain arrangements or patterns. Well, I have, for sometimes, I must tell you, been very occupied with what I have called 'interior landscapes.' You saw it lately reproduced – I don't have to tell you. Because the construction of the oldest apparatus of human thinking, where the creative idea comes from, it's very peculiar and very curious. There is our spine, brain goes in vertebrates terminate in a sphere called our skull, and there is where our thoughts and memory is. Besides that, the nerves, the sensory nerves, are for a quick, automatic, immediate reactions in our brain, in our brain in the hieratical reaction, in our sensory nerves,

immediate reaction. There we have the two different reactions. . . .
So you see there is the origin of the centrifugal running away and
centripetal moment in a psychic life. There is the order, often a new
order is misunderstood for disorder.

Gertrude Stein was very much interested in speed; she was always
very much annoyed because I was so slow. I have always an image about
myself that I am a turtle. I am very slow. Well, you will not believe, in
those drawings that you saw reproduced I sometimes was sitting for six
weeks. It is very long because some of my colleagues are doing twenty
a day. She was always surprised why I shouldn't go quick. She really
wanted me to be in someway as quick as automatic writing. Maybe my
hands were clumsy, but I was not thinking that way. I told you about
the time when I was in Paris the newest ideas were the investigation
of time by Bergson, the ideas about flow of time and continuity. (I
hope it doesn't bore you. I will tell you funny things sometimes, but
not always. You know, artists are not always funny – and the idea of
quality versus quantity, you are all bright, young men, you know it all.)
So there was a new element, time. I will tell you something that will
surprise you probably. I think Gertrude Stein was very little affected
by the ideas of Mr. Bergson. I think she went in a completely different way, and if she repeated, her mind was creating certain patterns.
Those patterns have to do with Platonic ideas of the archetype. You
know that all, you know Euclid, you know of the five perfect bodies,
et cetera. I don't have to speak about that to you, you know it all. For
me she created polyhedra in words, and their repetition and the number of repetitions, have to do something with that. She created new
relations between words, between the same words, and to come to that
deeper, purer, private meaning to the new freedom. Well, I give you
an example. Do you know the picture by Van Gogh called *The Chair*?
That poor, yellow, straw chair staying alone on the floor and that blue-
greenish background, probably a chair from an asylum. But that sort
of a chair is an object. But by Van Gogh it became so isolated that it

became *the* object, it became *the* chair. You understand when you stay in front of that picture in the Tate Gallery, which hangs next to his famous *Sunflowers,* you are feeling that you stay in front of a human being. You are really staying in front of Van Gogh, and this is what happens when [an] object is so isolated, so concentrated, so powerful that it loses that meaning that you can sit in it, because you cannot sit in chair Van Gogh, because it is an extraordinary being.

She used to speak a great deal and be interested in what is simplicity. What is stupidity? She told to me that the difference in people is never in intelligence, the most intelligent they are the more they are alike. You can't get higher than the Himalayas, but a mass of mountains in the chain of Himalayas, but you can be different, you can be less and less and less and less and less in stupidity. The stupidity is endless, stupidity is like an image of eternity, it has no end. She was saying that artists are different in their stupidity. And I was trembling whether I'm there, because she didn't know very many Russians before, and she was interested in Russian stupidity like she knew, excuse me, American stupidity, and English stupidity, and Italian stupidity, French stupidity, and German stupidity. But she thought French stupidity was very little stupidity, it was the less stupid stupidity. Therefore, she lived in France to be left alone. If you realized that she worked insistently, every day, to be published the first time by a real publisher, publishing house, after she was sixty. But I wonder who will do that, who will have the insistence, you understand the obsession, the surety, the purity of insistence to do that. No concessions. She used to tell me, 'Don't you ever dare to make concession. Then one walks, down, down, down, down.' There's no end of walking down. And I never made concession. Also, there were lots of traps set to me, to trap me in hats and dresses, in fashions and elegance. They couldn't, I was clumsy.

Well, she always when she spoke to us and to me, she would like very much people could listen to her. When you hear Virgil Thomson and he will tell you about 'Mother of Us All.' It is very wonderful opera and Susan B. Anthony is really Gertrude Stein, for me, because what she says is so much what Gertrude Stein used to say. 'Four Saints in Three Acts' [is] a wonderful dream, it's really the credo of Gertrude, four for mortal and three for divine. There you see her preoccupation with symbols of numbers, there we come to Pythagoras, there was come back again to Plato, and to Euclid and so forth. You know her motto, 'A rose is a rose is a rose is a rose.' You know that Dante spoke of the rose in which the divine word made itself flesh. It is the word of perfection, the word of human perfection. And in spite of all of that, in spite of thinking so deep, so pure, to working on finding that word, that out of that – instead of being a crock, a plate, a pitcher – would suddenly become a revelation of the same word. She was very simple, very jovial, very cordial, and very charming. In the difference with my other American friends who used to go in cafes, drinking cocktails and discussing and discussing till they didn't know what they were talking about, she was having teas. She had a few friends, and marvelous food and delicious things to eat, and the atmosphere of the rue de Fleurus with rosish walls, tall studio in the court. You have to pass the concierge and they will ask, 'Mlle. Stein, *s'il vous plait*, madame,' and she would say, '*Dans la cour, au fond, la porte a droite.*' And there was Gertrude Stein. The entry was like part of a lantern full of glass, and when you come in in the tiny hall there were lots of objects. You know Gertrude adored objects. There were peculiar objects. I remember a mirror that had a convex, round circular mirror in the middle and then lots of concave mirrors with equal circles around, like something very unusual like a toy. She looked [at] objects like toys. Here enormous amount of pictures. I can't give you any idea of what a lovely thing it was. It was about so high. . . . Most of them were Picassos. Above the mantlepiece was a little Cézanne. On one side was portraits of Gertrude Stein by Picasso, on the other side was the portrait of Mme. Cézanne, by Cézanne, in a green dress, a very wonderful portrait of extraordinary color achievement, maroon armchair and pale green dress with dark green velvet. Gertrude Stein used to tell me the story, how she was wanting to buy this portrait at an exhibition of Cézanne, and all the scandal that was connected with it, but I will tell you. She wanted to see an exhibition of Cézanne, but the dealer was Mr. Vollard. He was Martinique, he was rather dark colored, and he was very temperamental. So sometimes when he didn't want anybody to bother him, he was huge, enormous. He would stand across the door looking at the public, and no one dared to come in. And the pictures were never hung, all put around the walls. So Gertrude Stein came and didn't dare to enter because she thought he was furious – and she was not the kind of person who would be afraid of anything. So, then she came another time and she found him not standing at the door and she looked at all the pictures. She loved that picture and bought it. Then her family was very much annoyed and she got into a great deal of trouble because they thought she was mad to buy that kind of art. But she was very wise to buy that kind of art. She could not draw herself a thing. She told me, I think and I remember, she could not draw an elephant trunk. You know an elephant's trunk is not a straight line, it is not a special curved line, it is a flubby line; anybody could draw these lines, you know. But she couldn't. So, she was fascinated by art and by drawing – how it happened. I used to tell her, 'Do you write words very illegible?' I hardly could read. I, myself, writing awful, but she was writing so difficult besides it was in French. She had rather simplified French. So, I was very much puzzled about this interest about painting. She [said] she was fascinated by painting because she didn't know anything about it. And she told me that she was fascinated about what I was doing because she didn't understand what I was doing. She asked Juan Gris, my friend; he didn't know either. I didn't know very much myself. But now I know. You know, that's why when artists speak about their art, it is not interesting. Because what they do is interesting and later on they understand. If an artist decides a priori what he is going to do, he is not an artist. He's maybe a commercial artist, but he is not an artist. He is something else.

Well, I talk to you about her fascination about objects, because she felt that the latest idea in art, as shown in an object, came to an end. Well, I have to take you now very far. I have to take you to the beginning of our Christian era. Well, after the glory of the Roman fresco painting and Greek fresco painting which [we] considered in Italy, we consider in Pompeii, and the technique is so extraordinary that it is really like the late seventeenth century. They knew perspective; they did it very well. And Pompeii had painters, not of the first class. Pompeii was not even Miami. There were some palm beaches there, too, but it was not Pompeii. So, the great works didn't survive. But still in the minor works, the technique, the understandings of drawing. And then we see in the Roman catacombs one-line drawings, simple forms, mostly symbols, but the symbols which go way back, millenniums. From those lines and from those flat drawings which represent the new born idea of [the] Christian world, man was a part, a very tiny part, of the world of God. That was a new world, new religion, new idea. Man was included in a world of God, and the world of God was glorious. It was all gold, it was on a gold ground. And what is gold? Gold reflects light. Well, I will tell you something that will seem strange. Byzantine art had its subject and that was light. What you see in the object in Byzantine art had its subject and that was light. What you see in the object in Byzantine art is the symbol, but the subject of Byzantine art was light. Later on when the Byzantine passed into the idea of three-dimension art because the light fell on an object, that object was lit by light and half shadow. You never saw the shadow. You saw the shadow on the ground. The object was separated from the world of God. There is the separation of [the] world of men and [the] world of God. So, for about a thousand years the elaboration of art about the subject of art was space. (I am sorry, it probably bores everybody frightful, but I'm sorry. Doesn't matter. Somebody must be bored.) You see, this idea came to an end with the cubism (good heavens, I've talked too much already, and I will now come to the end), with the cubism, and it has to be born, a new idea, and from my point of view the new idea was all about time. So, I myself looking back on what I have done, think that all my researches were about time. Time is not time from New York to Chicago or time is money; this is all nonsense. It's not temporal time. It's a time in idea like space was an idea. And from my point of view, as strange as it seems to you, Gertrude Stein was in love with that idea of time, in the existence of objects, in existence in words, like people are in love with precious stones, where it becomes the world, when it becomes the most concentrated idea of the world. I want to tell you lots of things more, but I just won't – I have no time and you can see painters can talk you to slumber. And I hope you're not asleep. Anyhow, I think she came to what people think [of as] complexity and complications through her rhythms, to her idea of time completely new. You know, you are assisting at the birth of [the] idea of time. It will take [a] long time to liberate it, but one day, we'll not see it maybe, there will be again renaissance, there will be again Leonardos, there will be again Michelangelo and Raphael. We don't see it, but who cares? It will exist, this wonderful idea. Gertrude Stein brought [clarification] and not confusion. Because confusion is chaos, it's where before any order has begun. There is a great deal of confusion about art nowadays, and I'm not going to talk [about] it because I'm not talking about my art. You will have to find it by yourself. Look at it (for the time) who is doing and who is not doing well. But in my profession I know one miraculous name. You will be very much surprised. This name is Piet Mondrian. That man painted extremely simple panels, where on a seemingly white ground, divided by what seems to merely be black lines of different sizes and with some rectangles in color. If you sit in front of that picture or in front of any of his pictures, but you cannot see it quick, you see it certain times. You have to concentrate and suddenly in front of your eyes, the background recedes, the airy, wonderful structure is advancing towards your eyes and you see the green going far and the red coming nearer and the yellow going out of sight. And in front of your eyes is the structure. You are assisting at something that becomes in front of your eyes, that's veritably a becoming, you are assisting at the birth of a form. It is miraculous to recreate the form, but to make you see form being born in front of you – it is a great miracle. So, if you read Gertrude Stein in those repetitions of rhythms, those repetitions of forms you see the same thing . . . becoming of what – of style. Many will try to do it, many will work on it, but many worked on space, but Cimabue who started first and Giotto and Ucello and Fra Luca Pacioli, not speaking of Leonardo and Michelangelo and Raphael who created extraordinary works, developed the idea of space extraordinarily.

I think that Gertrude Stein was a very extraordinary symbolical figure. She was living in Paris, in France, in the center of the world, center of the world of art. She was well-known there. She was known there. She was translated there. She came to the United States already famous, very famous. She brought you the crown of art. It is an extraordinary moment to see, that crown of art which came from Egypt to Greece, from Greece to Rome, to Italy, to France, coming to your country. She brought you Aurora of art, humbly working, unpublished for many decades. Therefore, she was courageous. She was like a pioneer, like your ancestors, pioneers in the search of a new idea. Well, I came to an end and I hope you're not bored, and I will conclude my little talk which was very long for you with a few words which my friend, Charles Henri Ford, the poet, said in his poem called 'Ballade for Baudelaire':

> A wingless horse heard a story one day
> About a horse with wings
> And flew away.

HAROLD ACTON

'I was born in the twentieth century, which is closer to the ninth than the nineteenth, and I belong to no special movement. It is undeniable, however, that I love beauty,' Acton wrote, defending himself as a self-proclaimed aesthete. His appreciation of beauty began early, in the elegant Florentine villa where he grew up, a world that extended through the aristocratic mansion and into staid, manicured gardens where he and his older brother spent idyllic days. Only in summer did he leave the boundaries of this sumptuous environment, when he and his family sought to escape the heat of Italy by visiting his grandparents in Chicago and Lake Geneva, Wisconsin. Though he 'felt just as American as . . . English,' his strongest childhood memories stem from the glistening villa La Pietra.

Between childhood and Oxford, Acton was cloistered in a private school near Wokingham, Berkshire. 'My spirit rebelled and remained perverse until Oxford set me free,' he wrote, for he was never comfortable with his contemporaries and scorned their pranks and games.

At Oxford he felt more home, although his admiration for the Sitwells and T. S. Eliot set him apart from the more conventional scholars. 'Experiments with words fascinated me,' he admitted, and there were only two writers who earned his complete admiration – Joyce and Gertrude Stein.

When he learned from Edith Sitwell that Stein was to visit England, he invited her to address the 'Ordinary,' Oxford's literary society.

There was so much curiosity about the writer that Acton opened the
lecture to nonmembers; the audience filled a large room and listened,
rapt, as Stein recited 'Composition As Explanation,' 'casting a spell
with her litany.'

'The illusion that we were living in a continuous present was certainly there,' Acton remarked. 'When the reading came to an end life
moved considerably faster.' She was furiously assaulted with questions
as soon as she finished speaking, but she remained undaunted, answering them 'in reassuring motherly tones, patting and soothing the
obstreperous with gusty sallies.' She completely charmed the skeptical
and hostile, dispelling the popular image of her as 'a mermaid swathed
in tinsel, smoking drugged cigarettes.' To Acton, she seemed rather
like an Aztec priestess.

He visited her several times in Paris, where, Acton recalled, they
talked of his writing, or of Modernity (it was her 'religion . . . and she
harboured a notion that Great Britain suffered from hardening of the
arteries'), or, more likely, of China – Acton's obsession.

He speculated that Hans Christian Andersen's story, 'The Emperor's Nightingale,' first awakened in him an interest in China. In any
case, the interest developed into 'an innate love of China beyond ratio-
nal analysis. . . . Until I went to China my life would not be integrated
and I knew it.'

Finally, in 1932, he stood on Chinese soil for the first time. 'An immense calm descended on me. . . . I felt strangely at home.' He lived
in China for the next seven years, traveling, lecturing in English at
Peking National University, writing. It was not until 1939, when the
war spurred him to England to join the RAF, that he could bring
himself to leave. In the years that followed he devoted much time to
translating the plays of the Peking theater.

Though his love of things Chinese earned him a dubious reputation
among many of his countrymen, Stein understood his passions. 'Acton

is now a Chinaman,' she declared, '. . . I imagine he really does now really look and feel like a Chinaman. . . .' But his wide travels never took him to China again; instead, he returned to the villa La Pietra, to its garden, and to the 'vanished period' to which he belonged.

from *Memoirs of an Aesthete*

Bruised by the cold, we adjourned for a hearty luncheon at a Catalan *bistro* nearby where the Master was treated with becoming reverence. Though he let others do the talking he radiated contentment in a detached way special to celebrities. Dora Maar was a soothing presence, Marie-Laure an eloquent Muse. The Master purred. Gertrude Stein's name cropped up during the meal. She and Alice Toklas had just returned from exile in a taxi bearing her most cherished possession, Picasso's portrait of her painted in 1906 – together with her white poodle Basket and a large store of edible provisions.

'Let's all go and see her,' said the Master. So there was a grand reunion with everyone talking at once in the Rue Christine. Picasso hugged Gertrude like a beloved bolster. '*Et mon portrait?*' he asked with a sudden note of anxiety, as if it were a lucky talisman. How often had he raised that question since it had been painted? It was there waiting for him and he examined it minutely. 'Ah, it is finer than I had dreamt,' he said, embracing her again.

If only as a publicity agent Gertrude had brought him luck. Her brother Leo, who was as repetitive as he was deaf – there was a strong family likeness – had often told me that when he had bought the early Picassos 'she pretended to have discovered' Gertrude had been furious with him for buying such daubs. Be that as it may, she had revised her

From *Memoirs of an Aesthete 1939–1969* by Harold Acton. © 1970 by Harold Acton. Used by permission of Viking Penguin, a division of Penguin Books USA Inc.

first impression. Her article on Picasso in *Camera Work* (August 1912) begins: 'One whom some were certainly following was one who was completely charming.' After repeating this sentence with minor variations she proceeds: 'Some were certainly following and were certain that the one they were then following was one bringing out of himself then something that was coming to be a heavy thing, a solid thing and a complete thing.' The theme of 'something had been coming out of him' alternates with 'This one had always been working' – yet 'He was not ever completely working.' The longest sentence in the article attempts to summarize his achievement: 'This one was always having something that was coming out of this one that was a solid thing, a charming thing, a lovely thing, a perplexing thing, a disconcerting thing, an interesting thing, a disturbing thing, a repellent thing, a very pretty thing.' Later, in her best known and most lucid *Autobiography of Alice B. Toklas*, she paid him the supreme compliment of bracketing him with herself as a 'first class genius.'

It was amusing to watch the geniuses together. Both were rugged and squarely built; both had short hair and might have been taken for Aztec Mexicans; but whereas Picasso was muscularly mobile Gertrude was dumpily static. Though fifteen years had passed since I had seen her and Alice Toklas I could detect little change except that Gertrude had become more aggressively American in idiom and the use of slang, which seemed odd considering that she had been an expatriate most of her life. We had many friends in common and I saw her often. If one respected her colossal ego she could be warmly sympathetic. Her attempt to revitalize language was chiefly remarkable for its pertinacity, but only a fraction of her sense of fun percolates into her writings. Here and there a phrase arrests one's attention, such as 'Civilization begins with a rose,' but how many pages of stuttering repetition must be negotiated in order to find a gem of this quality!

In "Composition as Explanation" she wrote: 'For a very long time everybody refuses and then almost without a pause almost everybody accepts.' Almost everybody had accepted Picasso as a painter, but I fear that Gertrude Stein's 'continuous present' is already a thing of the past. Her *Three Lives* had influenced writers of Hemingway's generation.

Having complete faith in herself, she had some to spare for others. Her memory was retentive and she praised my long-forgotten fantasy, *Cornelian*. I might still become a good writer, she observed: I had plenty to say and could say it well if I forgot all about English literature and remembered that I was half-American. 'Your next book,' she added, 'must be a book of memoirs.' Eventually I took her advice. While she discoursed with much humour and sense in a placid voice Alice attended to domestic details, acted as interpreter and tactful go-between. Hemingway has hinted that Alice had a vicious side, but I never saw her other than gentle and devoted to Gertrude, whom she cosseted with creamy cakes.

I invited them to lunch with me at the Chatham and the Officers Club and in each place they created a sensation. John Cullen, who was often in the company of a pretty French girl – 'they are pretty like orchids, not like primroses,' he remarked of the women of Paris – was shocked by the extreme dowdiness of this elderly couple. Gertrude's billowing skirt was not low enough to hide a pair of woolen gaiters which fell about her ankles, and Alice, tiny and hunched beside her with a hooked nose and light moustache, reminded John of the maiden ladies who fusted at Bath or Cheltenham. Gertrude insisted on bringing her poodle Basket, which made them even more conspicuous among women who resembled sleek mannequins. But Gertrude carried herself with the assurance of a Cleopatra. John was soon won over by their conversation and remarked: 'I can see that I shall be calling Miss Stein "*chère maîtresse*" next time I see her.' When he mentioned that Hemingway was in Paris, Alice Toklas, speaking for both of them as usual, said the only thing they liked about him was his good looks when they first knew him at the age of twenty-four. They thought he had become hopelessly commercialized. 'But the *career*,' he once said to them. It was always 'the career . . .'

My American colleagues at the Chatham were thrilled to meet her and in a very short time she was distributing autographs in her sloping scrawl. This was my second guest who was asked for an autograph in public. The third was Norman Douglas in a Capri restaurant. 'Certainly not,' he snapped. 'Unless they're prepared to pay me a fee. Never heard of such cheek. They'll be forging my signature next. I've seen that happen before.' Had he been asked personally he might have obliged them, but they had sent the request by a waiter he disliked. For Gertrude the request was an outward and visible sign of her celebrity. Considering that she seldom went out except to take Basket for a walk, her intimate knowledge of other people's lives was astonishing: she excelled in the analysis of human relationships, yet her pen-portraits of Cocteau, Edith Sitwell and other friends contain no trace of her psychological insight. The repetition of 'Needs be needs be needs be near' conveys little of Cocteau whereas in conversation there was some truth in her remark that he prided himself on being eternally thirty.

An assiduous crony of hers was Thomas Whittemore, the Bostonian professor so comically sketched by Evelyn Waugh in *Remote People*. Although Berenson and many scholars deemed him a pious fraud, he had been responsible for the restoration of the Byzantine mosaics at Hagia Sophia and other mosques in Istanbul and had founded a Byzantine Institute in Paris which he had come to reopen. Under the Occupation it had become a shambles, he said, and he complained that the Ritz Hotel, where he was staying, was positively Siberian, and he kept running into that awful cad Hemingway (a fellow Ritzonian but not a Bostonian) who gave him the cold shivers. Recollecting the dire discomfort of his trip to the Abyssinian monastery of Debra Lebanos with Evelyn Waugh, I had to smile.

The professor was almost as enthusiastic about Gertrude as about

Byzantium and his flattery warmed the cockles of her heart. His articulation was painfully deliberate, but there was an ironical gleam in his eye which belied his solemnity. He told me that he had started cleaning the mosaics of Hagia Sophia with very fine dental instruments: 'I scraped them like ivory teeth with marvellous results.' Whatever his shortcomings, he deserved credit for this achievement. He gave me to understand that it had largely been due to his friendship with Mustafa Kemal, whom he had been able to influence in many constructive ways.

I doubt if the G.I.s who flocked to visit Gertrude had perused her writings. For them she was one of the living monuments of Paris, and they were attracted to this elderly frump as if she were a glamorous film-star. She must have felt like one when she posed for their cameras in front of the Stars and Stripes. She also felt fiercely democratic. This intellectual *vivandière*, as Natalie Barney called her, showed them her pictures, watched their reactions, encouraged any signs of independence, and scolded those who were fixed in their ideas. They sat on the floor and looked up to her with ravenous reverence while she spoke on a wide variety of subjects in a vigorous monotone, reducing them to speechlessness. I often wondered if and how she would influence their lives when they returned to the United States. Once I heard her explain to them that in her opinion all modern painting was based on what Cézanne had failed to do, instead of on what he had nearly succeeded in doing. To show what he could not achieve had become Cézanne's obsession and that of his followers, who had originated a system of camouflage which had developed into an art in peace and in war. Her argument was ingenious, but somewhat abstruse for the ingenuous, who listened open-mouthed, an occasional tongue displacing a gob of chewing gum.

When they were not calling on Gertrude and Picasso they were lining up for Chanel 5, the only scent in constant demand for transatlantic sweethearts.

BRAVIG IMBS

Bravig Imbs was one of the pleasant young men who could be found among Gertrude Stein's admirers in the years between the wars. When he met her in 1926, his claim to artistic achievement was the publication of a novel, *The Professor's Wife*, a somewhat realistic portrayal of the wife of a Dartmouth teacher. The woman's disturbance at the characterization prompted Imbs to leave the college. He came to Paris, where he found sympathy and friendship from such artists as Pavel Tchelitchew (Pavlik, in the selection), his sister Choura, René Crevel, and Georges Maratier.

For the five years during which his friendship with Gertrude Stein flourished, he was devoted and reverent. As Virgil Thomson recalled, Imbs was 'serviceable as an extra young man, good at errands, and pleasing in the home.' To amuse Miss Stein, he would play her favorite tune, 'The Trail of the Lonesome Pine,' on the violin. But even more agreeable to her were his letters, full of admiration and compliments, acknowledging her encouragement. 'You always remind me I am a person,' he once wrote, 'and then I feel better.'

But this warm relationship, like so many others for Gertrude Stein, was short-lived. According to Thomson, a close member of the Stein circle at that time, Imbs had made the mistake of bringing his pregnant wife to a boarding house in Belley, near Miss Stein's country home. Gertrude Stein, whose aversion to childbirth apparently was well known to everyone but Imbs, looked with distaste at the prospect of seeing Valeska Imbs through her pregnancy. Alice Toklas, as usual, solved the problem – she informed Bravig that the friendship was ended.

In 1944, more than a decade later, Imbs returned to Paris as a radio announcer, known throughout France as 'Monsieur Bobby.' Past difficulties forgotten, Stein greeted him warmly, but their friendship was rekindled only briefly; soon afterward Imbs was killed in an automobile crash.

from *Confessions of Another Young Man*

The day was Mardi Gras, and in some places on the Boulevards, people were courageously carrying on a Carnival; the weather was disagreeably damp and cold and the sky a sad, sad grey. I spent the best part of the afternoon shaving and washing and making sartorial preparations as though I were going to a ceremony.

I remember what difficulty I had selecting a tie and finally decided I had better dress as simply as possible, wearing a dark blue suit, white shirt, dark blue tie and handkerchief, dark blue socks, black shoes. But the combination seemed so sober and banal, I slipped a thin crystal bracelet . . . on my wrist, and then hastened off in a taxi to fetch Choura.

Choura was waiting for me calmly, pertly, wearing a stiff taffeta frock, and looking very pretty indeed with her brightly rouged lips. She really did have *le charme slav*. People turned to stare at her as we walked down the Boulevard Raspail.

Miss Stein's house, not far off, stood in a courtyard which always looked the same, summer and winter, paved in stone with an oval plot of evergreen plants in the center. I had become so panic-stricken by the time we reached the simple little door, with its window of ground

Excerpt from *Confessions of Another Young Man* (New York: Henkle-Yewdale, 1936). Reprinted in *Gertrude Stein: A Composite Portrait*, edited by Linda Simon (New York: Avon Books, 1974), 157–67.

glass, that I hastily slipped off the bracelet, feeling that it would be better to remain as simple as possible, and to say nothing.

In a moment, we had entered the bright little hall with its mirrors and umbrella vase and barometer and elaborate sconces, and I felt the servant's scrutiny as I took off my top coat. She was the famous Louise who had opened the door for Picasso, Matisse and Satie, and though she looked very stern and austere I was certain she liked me.

The entrance to the studio was by way of a very small painted grey door, and involuntarily one had to stoop, entering it. I remember the feeling of fatigue, mingled with my excitement, at the prospect of see-ing this important room. I am like a cat in that I can't be happy in a place new to me until I know all the doors and windows, the good chairs and the shaky one, the tables and the bibelots – especially the easily breakable bibelots – and the pictures on the wall. As one can-not politely go sniffing around the moment one enters a room for the first time, all the observation has to be done surreptitiously, and this is tiring.

Gertrude Stein had no such feeling. She was always changing the room about to the infinite annoyance of her sculptor friend, Janet Scudder, and myself, who both felt that furniture and objects should stay put in one place, once and for all. I would just get accustomed to a new arrangement and could devote myself unreservedly to conver-sation, when Gertrude would switch the chairs about again, involving most delicate calculations on my part as to the effect the new groupings would have on the guests and intimate friends.

Gertrude received so many people that she could not be bothered worrying whether they would get on together, but let all classes and kinds mix pell-mell and the devil take the hindmost. All she cared about was to shake loose the people who bored or annoyed her and though she was too kindly to drop them in the middle of a sentence, she always managed to introduce them to Alice before the sentence was ended. Alice acted both as a sieve and buckler; she defended

from *Confessions of Another Young Man*

Gertrude from the bores and most of the new people were strained through her before Gertrude had any prolonged contact with them.

That was why after the preliminary handshaking, I found myself taking very delicious tea and munching heavenly cakes with the gypsy-like person I had noticed with Gertrude at the gallery. She talked a blue streak. Without fluttering, or losing the trend of thought, or saying anything superfluous, Alice Toklas could keep up a most intense, elaborate and rapid flow of conversation. If you really listened you very quickly fell under the mild hypnotic state which her mental pyrotechnics induced, and then, with her brown eyes slightly glittering, she would dart questions like arrows, and in three minutes, would know your place of birth, your environment, your family, your connections, your education, and your immediate intentions. And she never forgot what she acquired. I remember, years later, when conversation would come to a dead center and Gertrude seemed to have nothing to say, I had only to ask some questions about an American family in Paris, and Alice would spend the rest of the evening giving their history with most complete and fascinating detail.

Of course, I did not realize exactly what was happening to me as I heard Alice talking about Mardi Gras being so much gayer in the old days, for I was too busy snatching stares to the left and right of me. Every square inch in the room was interesting, but it was so very softly lit by low table lamps and four magnificent candles in ornate silver sticks that I was hard put to make out certain objects, and the lovely blue Picassos, high on one wall, were all but invisible. Nevertheless, I was able to appreciate the perfect arrangement of the paintings – there must have been nearly a hundred of them – all hung close together and literally covering the walls. And yet no picture impinged on another, and each seemed in its proper place. There was no sensation of being in a museum either – the room had a distinctive life all its own – and that was, I suppose, due to the fact that each picture had its peculiar merit.

'Visiting Miss Stein is like visiting a school,' the Chilean painter, Guevara, said once to me, 'she has an example of every phase and period of modern painting and generally the best one.'

Of course, there was nothing sacrosanct about the arrangement of the pictures. Like the chairs, Gertrude shifted them about a good deal, and the Tchelitchews made way for the Tonnys and the Tonnys for the Francis Roses, but whichever way she shifted them seemed right. She did not lose herself in conjecture and experiment while doing this, as I would have done, but merely adopted certain pictures as pivots and grouped the other paintings about them. It was Elliot Paul who pointed out this procedure to me, simply because he was so fond of the chief pivot picture, the famed Picasso: a nude of a young girl, bearing a basket of flowers. It was one of the few paintings that Picasso had ever used a model for, and Gertrude so liked it when she first saw it that she bought it for a hundred gold francs. For my part, I preferred the nude that complemented it on the other side of the fireplace — tawny and Asiatic and darkly rose.

I had very little time that day, however, to look at the paintings the way I longed to, for I realized instinctively that Alice was important and required attention. My one idea, having arrived, was to be invited again, not out of any snobbishness, but because I knew Gertrude Stein could teach me a great deal about writing. So I nodded and yessed and noed while Alice Toklas talked on and on, and kept one ear strained to hear the conversation between Choura and Miss Stein.

Choura, genial, explosive, good humored, was recounting the departure of Allen and Pavlik for Tunis; how Pavlik had insisted on taking his easel and paints and brushes and canvases, so that he looked like Tartarin preparing for a lion hunt, and how Allen disappeared at the last minute to say good-bye to the grocer and give a farewell kiss to the girl at the creamery.

Gertrude began to laugh. She had the easiest, most engaging and infectious laugh I have ever heard. Always starting abruptly at a high pitch and cascading down and down into rolls and rolls of unctuous merriment, her hearty laugh would fill the room and then, as it gradually dwindled into chuckles and appreciative murmurs, the silence that followed seemed golden with sunlight. Her laugh was boisterous but I have never known it to offend even the most delicately attuned, for it was so straight from the heart, so human, so rich in sound.

I was startled when I first heard it that day, for like Sherwood Anderson, I, too, had foolishly expected a woman inscrutable and mysterious, and not this vital, headstrong and cordial personality. I was at once disappointed and relieved that such was the case, for though I was young enough to bear the divine heights more than five minutes at a time, it was much more agreeable to have to do with a human person.

Gertrude was very pleasant to me that day (for Alice finally let me go to her) but as she told me afterwards, judging from Pavlik's letter she thought I must be just another YMCA secretary and she had seen so many in the War that she never wanted to see any more of them. But, as she explained later to me, she had become puzzled at my answers which were not the answers she had expected, and to get this matter straight, to have me placed to her satisfaction, she decided on the spot to invite me again. When I heard her ask me to return, I was overjoyed and left with Choura, shortly after, treading on air.

Degrees of intimacy were very carefully graded in the Stein household and one was made to feel them keenly, so that when the first important degree was reached, that of being invited to lunch, one was all but overcome by this honor.

The supreme degree, of course, was a quarrel, and Allen, who had lunched and dined there and been invited to the Ain, and been sat with many, many times, was already planning for it.

'She's the greatest artist in the world,' he said, 'but, my dear, she has such a temper, such a temper! She has already had three violent quarrels with Picasso and I suppose ours is coming along.' He pretended to be resigned to the event but I could see that he did not find the prospect too unpleasant. I suppose that was the Irish in him.

At any rate, both Pavlik and Allen were very careful not to let me go alone to Gertrude's, for they held the balance of power in the salon and did not want it to be jeopardized. I had no such intention in mind, for I could not be attracted by the particular glory of such procedure, and, on the contrary, I was very glad that they chose to accompany me, for I had not completely recovered from my initial fright of Gertrude. Pavlik was delighted that I had found someone who inspired me with awe, for almost all the time I was with him, he was lecturing me, telling how insufferably young I was, how disagreeably persistent, how fundamentally vain and stupid. He recounted with malicious glee that Gertrude was not at all sure of me, and that she had found me 'rose dans tous les sens.'

Pavlik was painting my portrait then. He intended to paint three, the third to be mine, but after he had finished the first two he said it made him sick to look at my face any more and refused to continue. He was in a bad period at the time, and neither of the two portraits was any good. I was very disappointed, of course, and very depressed at all his scolding, but it had the effect of making me start work. I had to justify myself and so started writing some short stories.

I showed them to Gertrude, and she, with unerring accuracy, was able to point out the phrases, sentences and paragraphs where the literary intuition had been direct and pure, as well as those parts where substitution for the intuition had been made.

'You have the gift of true brilliancy,' she said to me, 'and less than anyone should you use crutch phrases. Either the phrase must come or it must not be written at all. I have never understood how people could labor over a manuscript, write and rewrite it many times, for to me, if you have something to say, the words are always there. And they are the exact words and the words that should be used. If the story does not come whole, *tant pis*, it has been spoiled, and that is the most difficult thing in writing, to be true enough to yourself, and to know yourself enough so that there is no obstacle to the story's coming through complete. You see how you have faltered, and halted, and fallen down in your story, all because you have not solved this problem of communication for yourself. It is the fundamental problem in writing and has nothing to do with métier, or with sentence building, or with rhythm. In my own writing, as you know, I have destroyed sentences and rhythms and literary overtones and all the rest of that nonsense, to get to the very core of this problem of the communication of the intuition. If the communication is perfect, the words have life, and that is all there is to good writing, putting down on the paper words which dance and weep and make love and fight and kiss and perform miracles.'

Gertrude had the secret of imparting enthusiasm to others, for as an artist, she was sincere and she felt deeply and she was bound up in her own writing, an humble subject in the kingdom of words. She rarely indulged in such outbursts, but generally marked with a faint pencil across the sentences or words which displeased her in my manuscripts and it was up to me to find out why they were wrong. When she did have something important to say, she said it rapidly, monotonously, almost with embarrassment; she much preferred to talk about baseball or the American doughboys or gardens or the cuisine of the Ain. It was then she could laugh and expand and radiate; writing for her meant discipline and duty and loyalties, all those elements in life which restrict and hamper.

'The words must be serried if the style is to be good,' she would say with a great deal of seriousness.

It was at such moments that Gertrude looked very like a monk, austere, illuminated, grave – the look monks have on their faces when they are officiating – and I remember the impression was even more striking after she had had her hair cut short. Pavlik almost went out of his mind for an afternoon on account of that incident. He had a

125

very easy classification of women: either they looked like his mother, his dear aunt or his sister. Gertrude had always looked like the dear aunt, and now with her topknot shorn away she did not look like any- one but herself – and Pavlik did not know where to place her. He had been planning for months to make her portrait, too – although always scared to death of the Picasso portrait which stared gloomily at him from the wall as if to say, just try to do better than I! – and now the shape of her head seemed quite changed and all his problems sprang up anew with fresh thorns. Of course, Pavlik was too polite to say what he really thought, but I think he could have choked Alice with pleasure for having played the barber.

It was at the beginning of the year and Gertrude simply felt she ought to make a change of some kind; Alice suggested cutting her hair as a way of passing that Sunday afternoon, and I must say she did it very well. Gertrude looked much more handsome, because her former coiffure had seemed somewhat Victorian, and this coiffure was at least modern.

Pavlik immediately went off the deep end when he saw her and then when he realized that Gertrude really wanted him to like it he com- posed himself enough to say that it really didn't make any difference. He never painted her portrait though he painted Alice's, as a kind of preparatory exercise. That painting was long and narrow and all in dull dark blues; it gave Alice a sleepy vulture look which was very strange.

Alice liked it but Gertrude did not, and Pavlik got out of that situa- tion by telling all his friends that Gertrude liked it but that Alice loathed it, loathed him, and set up such antagonistic vibrations that it would be impossible for him to paint Gertrude's portrait. It was not exactly that Pavlik had cold feet, but he was a Russian to the core, and it did distress him that he should be kowtowing to a Jewess.

Whenever that subject came up, Allen would unctuously pour oil on the troubled waters and say: 'Gertrude is the most un-Jewish person I ever knew. She is so dangerous and tolerant and has such a magnificent brain. Those aren't Jewish traits.' Pavlik would struggle a while and then would cede, saying, 'Yes, yes, Gertrude is magnificent, she knows so much about painting, she has such perfect taste and yet she can't draw a cow. That's wonderful.'

As a matter of fact, I don't think Gertrude knew much about paintings at any time. Her flair was for people and particularly for genius and she seldom erred. Her capacity for sizing up a person's character in a relatively brief time was of an uncanny precision – although Gertrude had nothing of the occult about her. She was always much more interested in the painter than in what he was doing and she measured his artistic worth by the amount of his resistance to her. She really had a great love for Picasso. 'When he was young,' she told me once, 'his black eyes would flash white fire' – but Picasso was as hard as nails and had a Spaniard's attitude towards women and never, never yielded. Gertrude was attracted to his genius, for it was so akin to her own, a Phoenix-like genius capable of incredible destruction and incredible invention, but when the exchange between them was not perfectly balanced there would be those violent outbursts of temper and subsequent separations.

To avenge herself, Gertrude would buy more Picassos and sell her Matisses. She finally sold all the Matisses she had, except a drawing of some flowers in a goblet, a most exquisite drawing which hung in her dining room and which I often coveted. Of course, it was Alice who was anti-Matisse, and whenever Gertrude was in the mood for selling she would urge her to dispose of the Matisses.

'He never knew what size canvas to use,' Alice would say to me with proper distaste.

I think Alice had a much surer feeling for painting than Gertrude, but very few people knew that, for it was always Gertrude who had the word in public. I remember the way they would barge down the rue de la Boétie in Godiva – that utterly charming wreck of a Ford which was about to be classed as a historical monument along with the taxis of the Marne, when it was affectionately relegated to a comfortable shed in Créteil – Gertrude driving with a stern expression and Alice sitting beside her, elegant and detached, as though she were in a victoria, on their way to an exhibition. They were always going to exhibitions (and there were new exhibitions in Paris every day) in their search for new human beings. Of course, it was very rarely that they found any painting that interested them sufficiently to seek acquaintance with the artist, and more often than not, the most interesting artists would make their way by themselves to the rue de Fleurus.

Gertrude's prestige was enormous, for she had undoubtedly been the only person in Paris to have faith in Picasso's sanity when he began Cubism. She bought the first two Cubist paintings Picasso created, pictures of a Spanish village, and everyone thought she had lost her mind. She continued adding to her collection, and Picasso sold her the best, for he was touched by her confidence. Years later, when the merchants began falling all over themselves to buy Cubist paintings, they saw the error of their ways and began to have a holy respect for Gertrude's opinions. She became an unofficial pontiff and the merchants dreaded her visits, for she could make or mar an exhibition with little more than a movement of her thumb. If she approved of an exhibition, she naturally carried off the best painting of the lot at a bargain price; if she disapproved, there was a whole coterie of American buyers who would follow her hint.

And so Gertrude's prestige as a modern art expert grew and grew, and all from the acorn of those two little Cubist paintings which she had purchased because she recognized Picasso's genius.

THORNTON WILDER

Thornton Wilder had visited Paris in the 1920s, often stopping in at Shakespeare and Company, where he seemed to Sylvia Beach 'rather shy and a little like a young curate.' But he met Gertrude Stein nearly a decade later, on the other side of the Atlantic, when he was a lecturer in comparative literature at the University of Chicago, where she had come to speak.

In Thornton Wilder, Stein found an advocate whose response to her work was both instinctive and unsentimental. She immediately recognized his 'serious beliefs and precision,' and her confidence in his opinions never diminished throughout their friendship. They spoke the common language of writers troubled by the same problems. 'The conceptions of Human Nature and the Human Mind . . . the relations of Masterpieces to their apparent subject-matter. Those things . . . and identity,' Wilder admitted, had 'become cell and marrow in me.'

These were the subjects of her lectures in Chicago, the problems she explored in *The Geographical History of America* and 'What Are Masterpieces and Why Are There So Few of Them?,' the questions they discussed when Wilder visited Stein in Paris and at her country home in Bilignin.

Wilder read Stein's work through the eyes of a scholar and wrote of them as one of America's most lauded artists. By the time he met Stein he had received the Pulitzer Prize for *The Bridge of San Luis Rey;* during the years he knew her he was awarded the prize twice again, for *Our Town* in 1938, for *The Skin of Our Teeth* in 1943. Still, he thought himself 'not an innovator but a rediscoverer of forgotten goods and I hope a remover of obtrusive bric-à-brac.' Like Stein, he found ideas 'in the great works of the past.'

His belief in her work insured her place in American literature and lessened the impact of the derision she suffered by so many. She was, Wilder felt, one of those rare minds who 'can . . . report life without adulterating the report with the gratifying movements of their own self-assertion, their private quarrel with what it has been to be a human being.'

He saw in her 'an impassioned listener to life,' just as he had always been. 'Neither her company nor her books were for those who have grown tired of listening,' he wrote. 'It was an irony that she did her work in a world in which for many reasons and for many appalling reasons people have so tired.'

from Introduction to
Four in America

Miss Gertrude Stein, answering a question about her line

A rose is a rose is a rose is a rose,

once said with characteristic vehemence:

'Now listen! I'm no fool. I know that in daily life we don't say "is a . . . is a . . . is a . . ."'

She knew that she was a difficult and an idiosyncratic author. She pursued her aims, however, with such conviction and intensity that occasionally she forgot that the results could be difficult to others. At such times the achievements she had made in writing, in 'telling what she knew' (her most frequent formulization of the aim of writing) had to her the character of self-evident beauty and clarity. A friend, to whom she showed recently complete examples of her poetry, was frequently driven to reply sadly: 'But you forget that I don't understand examples of your extremer styles.' To this she would reply with a mixture of bewilderment, distress, and exasperation:

'But what's the difficulty? Just read the words on the paper. They're in English. Just read them. Be simple and you'll understand these things.'

Now let me quote the whole speech from which the opening re-

From *Four in America* by Gertrude Stein (New Haven: Yale University Press, 1947), introduction by Thornton Wilder. © 1947 by Yale University Press, reprinted by permission.

mark . . . has been extracted. A student in her seminar at the University of Chicago had asked her for an 'explanation' of the famous line. She leaned forward, giving all of herself to the questioner in that unforgettable way which has endeared her to hundreds of students and to hundreds of soldiers in two wars, trenchant, humorous, but above all urgently concerned over the enlightenment of even the most obtuse questioner:

'Now listen! Can't you see that when the language was new – as it was with Chaucer and Homer – the poet could use the name of a thing and the thing was really there? He could say "O moon," "O sea," "O love" and the moon and the sea and love were really there. And can't you see that after hundreds of years had gone by and thousands of poems had been written, he could call on those words and find that they were just worn-out literary words? The excitingness of pure being had withdrawn from them; they were just rather stale literary words. Now the poet has to work in the excitingness of pure being; he has to get back that intensity into the language. We all know that it's hard to write poetry in a late age; and we know that you have to put some strangeness, something unexpected, into the structure of the sentence in order to bring back vitality to the noun. Now it's not enough to be bizarre; the strangeness in the sentence structure has to come from the poetic gift, too. That's why it's doubly hard to be a poet in a late age. Now you all have seen hundreds of poems about roses and you know in your bones that the rose is not these. All those songs that sopranos sing as encores about "I have a garden; oh, what a garden!" Now I don't want to put too much emphasis on that line, because it's just one line in a longer poem. But I notice that you all know it; you make fun of it, but you know it. Now listen! I'm no fool. I know that in daily life we don't go around saying "is a . . . is a . . . is a . . ." Yes, I'm no fool; but I think that in that line the rose is red for the first time in English poetry for a hundred years.' . . .

Distributed throughout Miss Stein's books and in the *Lectures in* from Introduction to *Four in America*

America can be found an account of her successive discoveries and aims as a writer. She did not admit that the word 'experiments' be applied to them. 'Artists do not experiment. Experiment is what scientists do; they initiate an operation of unknown factors in order to be instructed by its results. An artist puts down what he knows and at every moment it is what he knows at that moment. If he is trying things out to see how they go he is a bad artist.' A brief recapitulation of the history of her aims will help us to understand her work.

She left Radcliffe College, with William James's warm endorsement, to study psychology at Johns Hopkins University. There, as a research problem, her professor gave her a study of automatic writing. For this work she called upon her fellow students – the number ran into the hundreds – to serve as experimental subjects. Her interest, however, took an unexpected turn; she became more absorbed in the subjects' varying approach to the experiments than in the experiments them-selves. They entered the room with alarm, with docility, with bravado, with gravity, with scorn, or with indifference. This striking variation reawoke within her an interest which had obsessed her even in very early childhood – the conviction that a description could be made of all the types of human character and that these types could be related to two basic types (she called them independent - dependents and de-pendent - independents). She left the university and, settling in Paris, applied herself to the problem. The result was the novel of one thou-sand pages, *The Making of Americans,* which is at once an account of a large family from the time of the grandparents' coming to this country from Europe and a description of 'everyone who is, or has been, or will be.' She then went on to give in *A Long Gay Book* an account of all pos-sible relations of two persons. This book, however, broke down soon after it began. Miss Stein had been invaded by another compelling problem: how, in our time, do you describe anything? In the previous centuries, writers had managed pretty well by assembling a number of adjectives and adjectival clauses side by side; the reader 'obeyed' by furnishing images and concepts in his mind and the resultant 'thing' in the reader's mind corresponded fairly well with that in the writer's. Miss Stein felt that the process did not work any more. Her painter friends were showing clearly that the corresponding method of 'description' had broken down in painting and she was sure that it had broken down in writing.

In the first place, words were no longer precise; they were full of extraneous matter. They were full of 'remembering' – and describing a thing in front of us, an 'objective thing,' is no time for remembering. Even vision (a particularly overcharged word), even sight, had been dulled by remembering. The painters of the preceding generation, the Impressionists, had shown that. Hitherto people had known that, close to, a whitewashed wall had no purple in it; at a distance it may have a great deal of purple, but many painters had not allowed themselves to see purple in a distant whitewashed wall because they remembered that close to it was uniformly white. The Impressionists had shown us the red in green trees; the Postimpressionists showed us that our entire sense of form, our very view of things, was all distorted and distorting and 'educated' and adjusted by memory. Miss Stein felt that writing must accomplish a revolution whereby it could report things as they were in themselves before our minds had appropriated them and robbed them of their objectivity 'in pure existing.' To this end she went about her house describing the objects she found there in the series of short 'poems' which make up the volume called *Tender Buttons*.

Here is one of these:

Red Roses

A cool red rose and pink cut pink, a collapse and a
solid hole, a little less hot.

Miss Stein had now entered upon a period of excited discovery, intense concentration, and enormous productivity. She went on to writing portraits of her friends and of places. Two of her lectures in *Lectures in America* describe her aims in these kinds of work. She meditated long on the nature of narration and wrote the novel *Lucy Church Amiably*. This novel is a description of a landscape near Bilignin, her summer home in the south of France. Its subtitle and epigraph are: 'A Novel of Romantic Beauty and Nature and which Looks Like an Engraving . . . *"and with a nod she turned her head toward the falling water. Amiably."* '

Those who had the opportunity of seeing Miss Stein in the daily life of her home will never forget an impressive realization of her practice of meditating. She set aside a certain part of every day for it. In Bilignin she would sit in her rocking chair facing the valley she has described so often, holding one or the other of her dogs on her lap. Following the practice of a lifetime she would rigorously pursue some subject in thought, taking it up where she had left it on the previous day. Her conversation would reveal the current preoccupation: it would be the nature of 'money,' or 'masterpieces,' or 'superstition,' or 'the Republican party.' She had always been an omnivorous reader. As a small girl she had sat for days at a time in a window seat in the Marine Institute Library in San Francisco, an endowed institution with few visitors, reading all Elizabethan literature, including its prose, reading all Swift, Burke, and Defoe. Later in her life her reading remained as wide but was strangely nonselective. She read whatever books came her way. ('I have a great deal of inertia. I need things from outside to start me off.') The Church of England at Aix-les-Bains sold its Sunday School library, the accumulation of seventy years, at a few francs for every ten volumes. They included some thirty minor English novels of the 'seventies, the stately lives of colonial governors, the lives of missionaries. She read them all. Any written thing had become sheer phenomenon; for the purposes of her reflections absence of quality was as instructive as quality. Quality was sufficiently supplied by Shakespeare, whose works lay often at her hand. If there was any subject which drew her from her inertia and led her actually to seek out works it was American history and particularly books about the Civil War.

And always with her great relish for human beings she was listening to people. She was listening with genial absorption to the matters in which they were involved. 'Everybody's life is full of stories; your life is full of stories; my life is full of stories. They are very occupying, but they are not really interesting. What is interesting is the way everyone tells their stories'; and at the same time she was listening to the tellers' revelation of their 'basic nature.' 'If you listen, really listen, you will hear people repeating themselves. You will hear their pleading nature or their attacking nature or their asserting nature. People who say that I repeat too much do not really listen; they cannot hear that every moment of life is full of repeating. There is only one repeating that is really dead and that is when a thing is taught.' She even listened intently to dog nature. The often-ridiculed statement is literally true that it was from listening to her French poodle Basket lapping water that she discovered the distinction between prose and poetry.

It can be easily understood that the questions she was asking concerning personality and the nature of language and concerning 'how you tell a thing' would inevitably lead to the formulization of a metaphysics. In fact, I think it can be said that the fundamental occupation of Miss Stein's life was not the work of art but the shaping of a theory of knowledge, a theory of time, and a theory of the passions.

CECIL BEATON

Cecil Beaton, born in London in 1904, worked as a clerk and a typist before turning to photography in the late 1920s. Immediately, he earned a reputation as a photographer of the glamorous, the rich, and the famous, among them Greta Garbo, Edith Sitwell, and the Duchess of Windsor. Beaton became involved in theater as well, designing costumes for such productions as *My Fair Lady* and *Gigi*.

As Beaton tells us in his memoir, he frequently visited Stein and Toklas at Bilignin, where he admired their house and Alice's meticulous housekeeping. 'Each room,' he wrote in his diary, 'is as satisfying as the solution of a mathematical problem,' and in the bathroom, the soap was arranged 'in rigid, sharp-edged precision.'

After Stein's death, Beaton kept up his friendship with Toklas, contributing a recipe for 'Iced Apples (A Greek Pudding, very Oriental)' in her famous cookbook.

from *Photobiography*

My friendship with Gertrude Stein and Alice B. Toklas is also one that I owe to my camera. I had met these remarkable ladies in the company of Edith Sitwell in Paris on a momentous occasion when the three great literary figures became reconciled after a long bout of armed neutrality. I had been extremely impressed by the warmth and simplicity of this American couple, who showed such passionate interest in everything that was going on around them. But it was when they came to London for the first night of Gertrude's ballet, *The Wedding Bouquet*, that I first photographed them and, as a result of one long morning spent together in the studio, became a devoted admirer and deeply grateful friend of both Alice and Gertrude, who were like newly found fairy godmothers and gave me so much sympathetic encouragement.

When Gertrude and Alice arrived at my studio on that memorable summer morning, they at once displayed enormous delight in all the effects I had planned as properties and backgrounds for their special sitting. I had bought patterned wallpapers which, it transpired, were like those in their apartment in Paris. The twists of electric wire hanging from on high reminded them of a mobile Picasso had made for them.

They were quite a startling-looking couple; Gertrude with her closely cropped iron-grey hair, in her flowered waistcoat and tweed

138

skirt, Alice in a large black felt hat and grey flannel suit. In whatever juxtaposition I took them the effect was incongruous and strange; yet so great was the integrity of their characters that they could not possibly be made to look ridiculous. About Gertrude there was always something monumental. Her magnanimity shone through her trusting brown eyes, so that she was the best sitter any photographer could ever hope to have. I was able to take pictures of her at various stages of our friendship; I photographed her at Bilignin in her enchanting grey stone house among the poplar trees (where I stayed with her until the outbreak of war parted us), walking round the garden with Basket, her poodle, or rocking to and fro in her chair on the terrace while Alice did her needlepoint from designs by Picasso, prepared the salad for luncheon, or picked the hibiscus and tea roses for her very wonderful and personal flower arrangements.

After the long interval of war I went to seek out Gertrude and Alice in their apartment in Paris in the Rue Christine, and I was pleasantly surprised to find them both full of enthusiasm and none the worse for the experience of the dreadful years between. They were enthralled by the visits of a great number of G.I.s who had found their way there to pay their homage.

Gertrude said with evident pleasure in her warm nasal monotone, 'It's quite ex-tra-ordinary the way those boys come to see us. They come to see Pablo, and they come to see me. They don't go to anybody else, and I don't believe they come to see us because we're celebrities, but because we're rebels. They know Pablo and I have had to put up a fight in our time, and we've won, and that gives them a fellow feeling, and a link. They know we can understand their problems, and so, of all people in Paris, they come to Pablo and to me – and we're both very pleased they do – and we think that we can help them with their problems, in their loneliness and independence, and if they haven't got preconceived ideas that are too strong, then I think we can, and do, help them. But I tell some of them to do away. They've become set in their ideas, and I can't put up with anybody who has set ideas, with any who is *parti pris.*'

The most poignant photographs are of Gertrude taken on a few weeks before she died. She seldom talked of her illness, and her friends were not encouraged to enquire after her health; but she knew that she was very ill, and the photographs show how great a drain her illness had made upon her physique. In one, where she is leaning meditatively out from the window, it seems as if she were already looking into another world.

CLARE MORE DE MORINNI

Shortly before setting off on her U.S. tour, Gertrude Stein gave a spontaneous talk at the American Women's Club in Paris as a replacement for her friend Bernard Fay, who had been detained in Copenhagen because of bad weather. Stein had lectured only rarely before this talk, going to Cambridge, England in 1926, where she suffered from stage fright before her appearance. But her success there made her feel more comfortable about public speaking. She claimed, in fact, that her audience's acclaim made her feel 'just like a prima donna.'

Stein's talks usually ended with questions from the audience, to which she responded with wit and warmth. Since questions generally were her favorite part of her appearances, it is no wonder that she preferred this format when she stood in for Fay at the American Women's Club. Clare More de Morinni, chairman of the Club, records the surprised delight generated by Stein's talk, a reaction that was repeated many times during the U.S. tour.

Miss Stein and
the Ladies

It is rather rare to find anything off the record about Gertrude Stein. What with her articulate band of admirers, and her own power of putting herself across, there are few unreported aspects of even her daily life with Alice B. Toklas. But occasionally an unexpected episode pops up, such as Miss Stein's unheralded speaking appearance in December 1933, at the American Women's Club in Paris.

Lectures had helped make Gertrude Stein known to the wider world. Her first, undertaken with trepidation, was in 1926 before the University of Cambridge, the second with more confidence at Oxford. Both were highly successful.

But the appearance at the American Women's Club was purely spontaneous and unrehearsed. The Club had its ups and downs. At the moment its setting was a sumptuous mansion on the rue Boissière in the 16th arrondissement, a marble-floored gold-adorned building that had been the property of Dr. Serge Voronoff, the proponent of the so-called 'monkey gland rejuvenation' theory. Rather unfairly this seemed to diminish slightly the dignity of the house, but the handicap was bravely surmounted. It was very handsome, and the Club quite

First published in *The New Republic* (11 November 1967). Reprinted by permission of The New Republic, © 1967, The New Republic, Inc.

successful. Among its most interesting activities were the *causeries* by eminent and semi-eminent literary figures.

Mrs. Belloc-Lowndes, who wrote the story of Jack the Ripper, called *The Lodger,* had come from London to speak. Very small and plump and severely dressed in black, she had a surprising and disconcerting resemblance to Queen Victoria. Helen De Guerry Simpson came from London too. She had won an Australian Library Prize for a long and fascinating novel about a family's transition from Australia to England, also *The Spanish Marriage,* a picture of Mary Tudor. She was charming and died tragically in the blitz of the Second World War. Louis Bromfield and the Duchesse de Clermont-Tonnerre, among others, had represented literary Paris.

One such lecture, preceded by a large dinner party, was scheduled for the night of December 8, 1933, and I was to select the speaker. I chose the well-known French historian and critic, Bernard Fay, an authority on American history and the author of a biography of Benjamin Franklin; it seemed a most suitable choice for a Franco-American evening. Fay had accepted and had then asked that two of his friends, Gertrude Stein and Alice B. Toklas, be invited. This pleased me very much. I did not really know these two ladies, although I had met them in the American Library, then on the rue d'Elysée.

The evening turned out to be fairly snowy and stormy for Paris but nothing really alarming, and about seven-thirty guests began to arrive at the rue Boissière with stout wrapping over dinner coats and glittering evening gowns. A pleasant hum of conversation began as people warmed up with various drinks. Fay's two guests arrived and were looked at with the surprised interest their appearance always aroused: Gertrude Stein with her Roman emperor's head over stiff garments that seemed to be cut out of tweed, whether or no; Alice Toklas enigmatic and dark, with her slight resemblance, in spite of dangling earrings, to a Hebrew prophet. Miss Stein had a deep warm voice, seemed pleased at being there, looked about her, asked questions. Miss Toklas, in the flowered dress she often affected, said little and gave the impression of sizing one up.

But time was running out and no Bernard Fay. Eight-thirty came and went; still no speaker. I, as the chairman, felt butterflies in my stomach as guests began to wander toward the dining-room. It was a very handsome room, lit with crystal chandeliers and opening into a shadowy green winter garden, but it had never appeared so cheerless to my eyes.

Finally the committee went into a huddle and it was agreed that dinner should be served, and apologies made later to the speaker for having begun without him. At this critical moment the telephone rang and Bernard Fay's secretary's voice came through saying that he had had a telegram with the news that the historian was snowbound in Copenhagen. Obviously he was not to arrive that evening.

Sitting at the head table and wondering what next, I looked with gratitude on Monsieur Fay's friends. I slipped around to Alice Toklas between courses, and asked whether Miss Stein would take pity on the diners and speak afterwards?

Why not ask her?

So I asked and Miss Stein said firmly that she would answer questions. This was broadcast to the dining-room. There was a murmur of interest and satisfaction and people turned around to take a second look at Miss Stein.

The Autobiography of Alice B. Toklas had been published a few months before; the writer was already a celebrity. Thornton Wilder later said of her that during the war G.I.'s came to Paris to see Gertrude Stein and the Eiffel Tower. Miss Stein herself had written somewhere: 'I love to ask questions and I do not dislike answering them.' Now she was having a perfect opportunity to do both.

Miss Stein and the Ladies

I finished my dinner in peace and actually enjoyed it. We had a good chef, and now we had a speaker.

After dinner came the move to the ballroom, smallish for a ballroom but charming with its moulded gilded stucco and long windows with yellow brocade curtains. Then the evening really began. It turned out to be a far more exciting occasion than the original plan had promised. Questions came thick and fast.

'Is scrap iron with buttons on it Art?' was among the first. Miss Stein laughed. She had a wonderful laugh. I do not remember her answer, but it was all right. The evening was saved.

Some critics have since said that Miss Stein really didn't know much about art, that her associations with Picasso and Matisse, for instance, were merely fortuitous, due in great part to the purchases of her brother, Leo. But on that Saturday night, December 8, 1933, she had very convincing comments on the matter. The audience was delighted to find that she had an easy, outgoing platform manner, and could and did speak direct and lucid English.

There was one notable duel between her and Mrs. Harry Lehr, the widow of the legendary cotillion leader of vanished Newport. Mrs. Lehr, who had a magnificent mansion on the rue de St. Pères. It was filled with furniture and *objets d'art* of the 17th century, and obviously, in Mrs. Lehr's opinion, no art worth speaking about had ever appeared since the reign of the Roi Soleil. She alluded with fervor to Hyacinthe Rigaud and ermine mantles, and Largillière and frills. Gertrude Stein countered with Picasso and Braque. There could be no compromise, no meeting of minds, and the lively interchange was punctuated by bursts of laughter and applause. In the end, Mrs. Lehr, either routed or enraged, left with a swish of black chiffon and a glitter of diamond bracelets. But the questions went right on.

The evening was a huge success and was reported on the front page of the *New York Herald Tribune* the next morning under the heading,

'Gertrude Stein Meets Hecklers in Art Session at Women's Club.'

The account began: 'Gertrude Stein stepped into the breach last night at the American Women's Club as pinch-hitting speaker when Professor Bernard Fay found himself unavoidably detained in Copenhagen.' The *Herald Tribune* went on: 'Miss Stein began by saying, "I am unprepared to speak, but I will answer questions".'

'Why don't modern artists paint things as they see them?' This query came with others, from different parts of the room at almost the same time. Miss Stein took a deep breath.

'They try to paint the compositions before them as they do see them,' she explained. 'Human beings do not change, but the picture of the age before our eyes changes. The creative artist, whether he be an inventor like Wilbur Wright, or a painter, senses the change and tries to show the public what he sees.'

'The modern artist or writer is not just trying to astonish the world. Otherwise no sane person would work for years like a dog just to achieve the contempt of the greater part of the public.' She was obviously thinking about her own work.

'Maybe they're not sane!' came a shout from the audience.

'Oh, don't be silly!' exclaimed Miss Stein gently. She gave the impression of patting her heckler on the head.

She went on, as the *Herald Tribune* indicated: 'The point is the creative artist is always alone with his idea. The question of the public is only vanity. After he has done his work, he may be hurt by others' mockery, or pleased with their applause. But the onlookers, who see the changes in contemporary composition, but can't understand them, don't count.'

Some of the audience was wondering whether it 'counted' or not.

'Most people live in their epoch in that they understand ordinary things, such as steam heat and automobiles, but insist upon living in the past in matters of the intellect.'

This seemed true; but the pronouncement was followed by protestations, applause, congratulations and vehement denials. The evening ended in the warmest atmosphere of spirited controversy.

The next high spot for the chairman was being invited to tea to sample one of Miss Toklas' wonderful cakes. The two friends were still living on the rue de Fleurus. The cake *was* wonderful, but more interesting were the pile of little *cahiers* on the desk, the notebooks of French schoolchildren in which Gertrude Stein wrote her work. On the table were the skeins of wool and silk that would go into the petit point tapestry designed by Picasso, and destined for the little Louis xv armchairs or *chauffeures*. But best of all, Picasso's portrait of Gertrude Stein still hung on the wall. There she was, leaning forward, eyes intent, hair still long and arranged in a brown coil, a plain dark dress. It was very impressive. What a piece of luck I have had, I thought to myself. The invitation to tea was followed by an even more enchanting one, to lunch at Bilignin Belley (Ain) a summer home. The postcard on which the invitation was written, with a lopsided completely unrealistic view of the house there, painted by Sir Francis Rose, I only received on getting back to the United States. But Carl van Vechten furnished photographs of Bilignin: Gertrude Stein working in box-bordered flower beds with a small black dog named Byron looking on, or Gertrude sitting on the stone wall of the garden with the white poodle, Basket, beside a rose-covered '*gloriette*.' This was set against a misty landscape, accented by rows of poplars, so perfectly French and so satisfying.

One can only wonder what Fay thought of it all when he finally escaped from Copenhagen. But he was fond of Gertrude Stein and had said 'the greatest, most beautiful of her gifts is her presence.' He could only have been delighted.

T. S. MATTHEWS

Thomas Stanley Matthews was born in 1901 in Cincinnati, 'A grimy little city,' as he described it, where his father was an Episcopal minister. He was raised in the more affluent suburb of Glendale, supported not by his father's wages as a minister, but by his mother's considerable fortune as an heiress of the Procter family, of Procter & Gamble. 'All my immediate family,' he wrote, were 'directly connected with P&G, either by marriage or paycheck.'

After graduating from St. Paul's School and Princeton, Matthews went to New York to work as a journalist, first at *The New Republic* under Edmund Wilson, and later at *Time,* where he served as editor under Henry Luce. During his long career as a journalist he met many eminent figures, including Sir Winston Churchill, Albert Einstein, Whittaker Chambers, and, not least, Gertrude Stein, who he met during her American lecture tour in 1934–35.

He recalled many of these figures in a collection of memoirs titled *Angels Unawares,* explaining that certain people one meets seem to be, if not angels, then certainly messengers who urge us to reconsider the world around us. What is the message that these 'angels' bring? 'That . . . is impossible for me to tell,' Matthews admitted. 'As some professor has almost said, the message is the mystery. Whatever the message was, and whether we understand it or not, it must have been, to someone's mind, worth sending.'

Gertrude Stein

The first glimpse you get of her, as she trudges resolutely up onto the lecture platform, is reassuring. This solid, elderly woman, dressed in no-nonsense rough-spun clothes, seems at once smaller and more human than her monumental photographs or Jo Davidson's squat image of her. As she looks out over the audience and thanks us, with a quick low hoot of laughter, for 'controlling yourselves to five hundred,' we laugh too, in appreciative relief, and settle back in our seats to give her the once-over. This Gertrude Stein woman may not be so crazy, after all. Some of our wariness eases off. She has made a good beginning; there's no denying that.

But why are we here? Well, there are two answers to that question. Miss Stein knows one; we know the other. She knows we have come because we are interested – not so much in her as in her writing. We know better. We are here because we are curious – not so much about her writing, which we have never read, and probably never will, as about herself – an apparently sensible, perhaps really sane woman who has spent most of her life writing absolute balderdash, and then, by gum, a year ago published a book that was perfectly plain sailing and got her on the best-seller lists. We want to see what this creature looks like; we want to hear what she has to say for herself.

From *Angels Unawares* by T. S. Matthews (Boston: Ticknor & Fields, 1985).

Now that we can get a good look at her face, that too is reassuring. The photographs we have seen didn't show those deep black eyes that make her graven face and its archaic smile come alive. Her short-cropped hair doesn't look queer; it looks as right as a cap on a grandmother. And though this is her first visit home in thirty-one years, her voice is as unmistakably American – she says 'Amorrican' – as any of ours. As we listen to her low-pitched, harshly pleasant sound, we realize, with further grateful relief, that we were afraid she might have added, on top of her swami-like incomprehensibility, some of the affected patter of the expatriate. But no, we can see right away that she is too stubborn to have done anything like that. Foreign parts of speech have not affected her at all: she talks in as flatly sensible an American tone as any Midwestern aunt. We also notice with approval that she indulges in no gestures, except the natural, grandmotherly one of taking her pince-nez off and putting them on, and we soon discover, with mixed feelings, that she is not a very good lecturer: she drops her voice at the end of every sentence and talks more and more to one side of the room, so that a good third of us have to cup our ears and guess at the words we miss.

She is talking about herself, trying to explain what she has been up to all this time, and how she happens to write the way she does. It all sounds very sensible at first. She writes, she says, just the way she talks, and she tries to prove it by reading progressive examples from her books. But immediately, with the very first example, we notice a difference. That tonelessness that helps to lend an idiotic quality to her writing is emphatically absent from her reading. She reads, indeed, with an exaggerated emphasis, putting back all the italics and commas and dashes she has carefully not written. The passages she reads make startlingly good sense. A great light begins to break over us: by knowing what to accent, where to pause, we too might dig some meaning out of Gertrude Stein. It isn't true, then, that all that work of hers is just a brier patch; there *is* a rose in there, after all. A few of us make a mental note to try reading *Tender Buttons*, say, aloud – in the strictest privacy. Something might come of it.

Quite soon she says something funny. We laugh, not very loudly, and then look aghast. Was it meant to be funny? But Miss Stein doesn't seem to mind; she is even smiling herself. What a relief! We undo another tender mental button, and laugh whenever we feel like it. Toward the end of the lecture a few of us are shaking hysterically, and at the least excuse. But she doesn't seem to notice, and most of us are still sitting solemnly enough. After the lecture she is surrounded by an apparently reverent semicircle of undergraduates, who want to know still further. Her face a little flushed now from so much talking, she answers their questions with dogmatic directness. Yes, she considers herself a genius. No, self-expression has nothing to do with it. No, it is not her job to make people understand what she writes. Yes, she feels just like everybody else; she has often said to Picasso, who is also a genius, 'Do you feel any different from anybody else?' and no, neither does he.

The total impression we carry away is that of a fundamentally serious, not to say megalomaniac writer – are all really serious people megalomaniacs? – who has come back home for a visit in the happy consciousness that she has triumphed at last. Her own country, after thirty years of neglect, is delighting to honor her. Later, when you hear her in a fifteen-minute 'interview' on the radio, that impression is further confirmed. Miss Stein is having a swell time, wish young Miss Stein could be here too. She loves the tall buildings, the people on the street, she had a grand time at the football game, America is certainly a wonderful country. Miss Stein is decidedly bullish on America; her enthusiasm is delightful – a delighted visitor's enthusiasm. And she really seems to believe that we have hailed her as a genius, not welcomed her as a freak. She tells her 'readers' not to worry so much about understanding her. If you enjoy a thing, you understand it, she says; and she wouldn't be read if she weren't enjoyed; therefore her readers understand her. Unfortunately this pretty piece of logic blinks the fact that practically nobody does read her. Some of us may have sat through *Four Saints in Three Acts* (we went either to have a good laugh or to feel snobbish), or we have read what the newspapers have to say about her, or perhaps *The Autobiography of Alice B. Toklas,* or we have taken one horrified or amused dip into one of her serious books – but if we did, we hardly stayed in a minute; the water was too cold and there were too many queer fish around.

There is certainly some grudging admiration in our welcome to Gertrude Stein; even Republicans thought more of Upton Sinclair after the scare he gave them in California. We are Greek enough to reverence (or fear) as well as gibe at what we do not understand. Our intolerant, cocksure skepticism always wavers in the face of quiet certainty. But Miss Stein has been away a long time. She thinks we are polite. She is wrong: we are simply timid, unsure of our ground, unsure of hers as well. There are a lot of things in the world we don't know anything about, and she may be one of them. This incommunicable meaning of hers may even be important. Why not? – especially if the meanings we have been able to communicate with have one by one proved unimportant, meaningless, or false. And so we totter reverently from her presence and explode with laughter just outside the door. That doesn't mean, of course, that our reverence is any more fake than our laughter.

What Miss Stein does not seem to have gathered is that our altars to the Unknown God – and they are many – are at the same time sideshows, with the barker-priests always drumming up trade. If she really thinks, as she seems to, that the guarantee of her genius is the popular notice she is receiving here, she would do well to let another thirty years elapse before she tries it again. By that time she may have learned that newsboys don't care what they're shouting about as long as they sell their papers.

JOHN HYDE PRESTON

In 1934, Gertrude Stein sailed from Paris to her native America for her first stateside visit in more than twenty-five years. The trip, however, was not a sentimental return to her roots; it was, instead, a well-planned lecture tour designed to sell Gertrude Stein as a 'personality.'

Stein was excited by the idea that she would be lionized in her native land, but she was strict about her requirements: She was not to be introduced at her lectures. Because she did not like to eat in public, she would not attend luncheons or dinners in her honor. She asked a fee of one hundred dollars from schools, two hundred fifty dollars from clubs. And tickets sold for the lectures were not to benefit any cause.

She did not, however, limit interviews or photographs, and as she crossed the country from New York to California, she was eager to share her ideas about life and literature with journalists from large and small newspapers and magazines.

John Hyde Preston was a twenty-eight-year-old Canadian writer when he interviewed Stein in Manhattan. Later the author of *Revolution, 1776*, Preston saw himself as a debunker of cultural myths. Perhaps he believed that Stein, who had created her own self-serving legends, needed to be heard with a bit of skepticism. But, as this memoir shows, Preston was won over by Stein's directness, honesty, and volubility.

A Conversation with Gertrude Stein

She talks freely and volubly and sometimes obscurely, as if she had something there that she was very sure of and yet could not touch it. She has that air of having seen in flashes something which she does not know the shape of, and can talk about, not out of the flashes but out of the spaces between when she has waited.

I do not mean that there is in her conversation any trace of that curious obscurity which dims so much of her prose, for me at least – and I was frank (without wanting to be) in telling her that I could only guess sometimes at the written words. She seems peacefully resigned to the attacks that have been made upon her all her life and she has that air, so rare in writers, of living outside of both fame and criticism.

II

. . . 'You will write,' she said, 'if you will write without thinking of the result in terms of a result, but think of the writing in terms of discovery, which is to say that creation must take place between the pen and the paper, not before in a thought or afterwards in a recasting. Yes, before in a thought, but not in careful thinking. It will come if it is there and if you will let it come, and if you have anything you will get a sudden creative recognition. You won't know how it was, even what

First published in 'A Conversation,' *The Atlantic Monthly* (August 1935: 187–94).

it is, but it will be creation if it came out of the pen and out of you and not out of an architectural drawing of the thing you are doing. Technique is not so much a thing of form or style as the way that form or style came and how it can come again. Freeze your fountain and you will always have the frozen water shooting into the air and falling and it will be there to see – oh, no doubt about that – but there will be no more coming. I can tell how important it is to have that creative recognition. You cannot go into the womb to form the child; it is there and makes itself and comes forth whole – and there it is and you have made it and have felt it, but it has come itself – and that is creative recognition. Of course you have a little more control over your writing than that; you have to know what you want to get; but when you know that, let it take you and if it seems to take you off the track don't hold back, because that is perhaps where instinctively you want to be and if you hold back and try to be always where you have been before, you will go dry.

'You think you have used up all the air where you are, Preston; you said that you had used it up where you live, but that is not true, for if it were it would mean that you had given up all hope of change. I think writers *should* change their scenes; but the very fact that you do not know where you would go if you could means that you would take nothing truly to the place where you went and so there would be nothing there until you had found it, and when you did find it, it would be something you had brought and thought you had left behind. And that would be creative recognition, too, because it would have all to do with you and nothing really to do with the place.'

But what if, when you tried to write, you felt stopped, suffocated, and no words came and if they came at all they were wooden and without meaning? What if you had the feeling you could never write another word?

'Preston, the way to resume is to resume,' she said laughing. 'It is the only way. To resume. If you feel this book deeply it will come as deep as your feeling is when it is running truest and the book will never be truer or deeper than your feeling. But you do not yet know anything about your feeling because, though you may think it is all there, all crystallized, you have not let it run. So how can you know what it will be? What will be best in it is what you really do not know now. If you knew it all it would not be creation but dictation. No book is a book until it is done, and you cannot say that you are writing a book while you are just writing on sheets of paper and all that is in you has not yet come out. And a book – let it go on endlessly – is not the whole man. There is no such thing as a one-book author. I remember a young man in Paris just after the war – you have never heard of this young man – and we all liked his first book very much and he liked it too, and one day he said to me, "This book will make literary history," and I told him: "It will make some part of literary history, perhaps, but only if you go on making a new part every day and grow with the history you are making until you become a part of it yourself." But this young man never wrote another book and now he sits in Paris and searches sadly for the mention of his name in indexes.'

III

Her secretary came in and out of the room, putting things away in a trunk that stood open at the end of the couch (they sail to-morrow noon), exchanging a few words in a voice that was new for its softness; and suddenly out of something that we were saying about America came the discovery that both she and I were from Seattle and that she had known my father when he was a young man and before he went into the Klondike. And then as her secretary spoke a strange deep kinship of land seemed to take possession of the other woman, – who had been born in Pennsylvania and raised in Oakland, California, and had been in far-off Paris for thirty years without sight of her native earth, – for she began to speak with deep-felt fervor of her American experience in the past six months.

'Preston,' she said, 'you were saying that you had torn up roots ten years ago and tried to plant them again in New England where there was none of your blood, and that now you have a feeling of being without roots. Something like that happened to *me*, too. I think I must have had a feeling that it had happened or I should not have come back. I went to California. I saw it and felt it and had a tenderness and a horror too. Roots are so small and dry when you have them and they are exposed to you. You have seen them on a plant and sometimes they seem to deny the plant if it is vigorous.' She paused when I lit a cigarette; I could not make out whether she had been alarmed at my smoking so much or whether she was instinctively silent in the face of any physical activity on the part of her listener. 'Well,' she went on, 'we're not like that really. Our roots can be anywhere and we can survive, because if you think about it, we take our roots with us. I always knew that a little and now I know it wholly. I know because you can go back to where they are and they can be less real to you than they were three thousand, six thousand miles away. Don't worry about your roots so long as you worry about them. The essential thing is to have the feeling that they exist, that they are somewhere. They will take care of themselves, and they will take care of you too, though you may never know how it has happened. To think only of going back for them is to confess that the plant is dying.'

'Yes,' I said, 'but there is something more. There is the hunger for the land, for the speech.'

'I know,' she said almost sadly. 'America is wonderful!' Then without any warning she declared: 'I feel now that it is my business here. After all, it *is* my business, this America!' And she laughed with a marvelous heartiness, a real lust. When I asked her if she would come back she looked up slyly and was smiling still and she opened and shut her eyes with the same zestful expression with which a man smacks his lips.

'Well,' I said, 'you have had a long time to look. What is it that happens to American writers?'

'What is it you notice?'

'It is obvious. They look gigantic at first. Then they get to be thirty-five or forty and the juices dry up and there they are. Something goes out of them and they begin to repeat according to formula. Or else they grow silent altogether.'

'The trouble is a simple one,' she said. 'They become writers. They cease being creative men and soon they find that they are novelists or critics or poets or biographers, and they are encouraged to be one of those things because they have been very good in one performance or two or three, but that is silly. When a man says, "I am a novelist," he is simply a literary shoemaker. If Mr. Robert Frost is at all good as a poet, it is because he is a farmer – really in his mind a farmer, I mean. And there is another whom you young men are doing your best – and very really your worst – to forget, and he is the editor of a small-town newspaper and his name is Sherwood Anderson. Now Sherwood' – he was the only man she called by his first name, and then affectionately – 'Sherwood is really and truly great because he truly does not care what he is and has not thought what he is except a man, a man who can go away and be small in the world's eyes and yet perhaps be one of the very few Americans who have achieved that perfect freshness of creation and passion, as simple as rain falling on a page, and rain that fell from him and was there miraculously and was all his. You see, he had that *creative recognition,* that wonderful ability to have it all on paper before he saw it and then to be strengthened by what he saw so that he could always go deep for more and not know that he was going. Scott Fitzgerald, you know, had it for a little while, but – not any more. He is an American Novelist.'

A Conversation with Gertrude Stein

'What about Hemingway?' I could not resist asking her that question. Her name and the name of Ernest Hemingway are almost inseparable when one thinks of the Paris after the war, of the expatriates who gathered around her there as a sibyl. 'He was good until after *A Farewell to Arms*.'

'No,' she said, 'he was not really good after 1925. In his early short stories he had what I have been trying to describe to you. Then – Hemingway did not lose it; he threw it away. I told him then: "Hemingway, you have a small income; you will not starve; you can work without worry and you can grow and keep this thing and it will grow with you." But he did not wish to grow that way; he wished to grow violently. Now, Preston, here is a curious thing. Hemingway is not an American Novelist. He has not sold himself and he has not settled into any literary mould. Maybe his own mould, but that's not only literary. When I first met Hemingway he had a truly sensitive capacity for emotion, and that was the stuff of the first stories; but he was shy of himself and he began to develop, as a shield, a big Kansas City-boy brutality about it, and so he was "tough" because he was really sensitive and ashamed that he was. Then it happened. I saw it happening and tried to save what was fine there, but it was too late. He went the way so many other Americans have gone before, the way they are still going. He became obsessed by sex and violent death.'

She held up a stubby forefinger. 'Now you will mistake me. Sex and death are the springs of the most valid of human emotions. But they are not all; they are not even all emotion. But for Hemingway everything became multiplied by and subtracted from sex and death. But I knew at the start and I know better now that it wasn't just to find out what these things were; it was the disguise for the thing that was really gentle and fine in him, and then his agonizing shyness escaped into brutality. No, now wait – not real brutality, because the truly brutal man wants something more than bull-fighting and deep-sea fishing and elephant killing or whatever it is now, and perhaps if

159

Hemingway were truly brutal he could make a real literature out of those things; but he is not, and I doubt if he will ever again write truly about anything. He is skillful, yes, but that is the writer; the other half is the man.'

I asked her: 'Do you really think American writers are obsessed by sex? And if they are, isn't it legitimate?'

'It is legitimate, of course. Literature – creative literature – unconcerned with sex is inconceivable. But not literary sex, because sex is a part of something of which the other parts are not sex at all. No, Preston, it is really a matter of tone. You can tell, if you can tell anything, by the way a man talks about sex whether he is impotent or not, and if he talks about nothing else you can be quite sure that he is impotent – physically and as an artist too.

'One thing which I have tried to tell Americans,' she went on, is that there can be no truly great creation without passion, but I'm not sure that I have been able to tell them at all. If they have not understood it is because they have had to think of sex first, and they can think of sex as passion more easily than they can think of passion as the whole force of man. Always they try to label it, and that is a mistake. What do I mean? I will tell you. I think of Byron. Now Byron had passion. It had nothing to do with his women. It was a quality of Byron's mind and everything he wrote came out of it, and perhaps that is why his work is so uneven, because a man's passion is uneven if it is real; and sometimes, if he can write it, it is only passion and has no meaning outside of itself. Swinburne wrote all his life about passion, but you can read all of him and you will not know what passions he had. I am not sure that it is necessary to know or that Swinburne would have been better if he had known. A man's passion can be wonderful when it has an object which may be a woman or an idea or wrath at an injustice, but after it happens, as it usually does, that the object is lost or won after a time, the passion does not survive it. It survives only if it was there before, only if the woman or the idea or the wrath was an incident in the passion and not the cause of it – and that is what makes the writer.

'Often the men who really have it are not able to recognize it in themselves because they do not know what it is to feel differently or not to feel at all. And it won't answer to its name. Probably Goethe thought that *Young Werther* was a more passionate book than *Wilhelm Meister,* but in *Werther* he was only describing passion and in *Wilhelm Meister* he was transferring it. And I don't think he knew what he had done. He did not have to. Emerson might have been surprised if he had been told that he was passionate. But Emerson really had passion; he wrote it; but he could not have written *about* it because he did not know about it. Now Hemingway knows all about it and can sometimes write very surely about it, but he hasn't any at all. Not really any. He merely has passions. And Faulkner and Caldwell and all that I have read in America and before I came. They are good craftsmen and they are honest men, but they do not have it.'

IV

I have never heard talk come more naturally and casually. It had none of the tautness or deadly care that is in the speech of most American intellectuals when they talk from the mind out. If sometime you will listen to workingmen talking when they are concentrated upon the physical job at hand, and one of them will go on without cease while he is sawing and measuring and nailing, not always audible, but keeping on in an easy rhythm and almost without awareness of words – then you will get some idea of her conversation.

'Well, I think Thomas Wolfe has it,' I said. 'I think he really has it – more than any man I know in America.' I had just read *Of Time and the River* and had been deeply moved.

'I read his first book,' she said, misnaming it. 'And I looked for it, but I did not find it. Wolfe is a deluge and you are flooded by him, but if you want to read carefully, Preston, you must learn to know how you are flooded. In a review I read on the train Wolfe was many things and among them he was Niagara. Now that is not so silly as it sounds. Niagara has power and it has form and it is beautiful for thirty seconds, but the water at the bottom that has been Niagara is no better and no different from the water at the top that will be Niagara. Something wonderful and terrible has happened to it, but it is the same water and nothing at all would have happened if it had not been for an aberration in one of nature's forms. The river is the water's true form and it is a very satisfactory form for the water and Niagara is altogether wrong. Wolfe's books are the water at the bottom and they foam magnificently because they have come the wrong way, but they are no better than when they started. Niagara exists because the true form ran out and the water could find no other way. But the creative artist should be more adroit.'

'You mean that you think the novel form has run out?'

'Truly – yes. And when a form is dead it always happens that everything that is written in it is really formless. And you know it is dead when it has crystallized and everything that goes into it must be made a certain way. What is bad in Wolfe is made that way and what is good is made very differently – and so if you take what is good, he really has not written a novel at all.'

'Yes – but what difference does it make?' I asked her. 'It was something that was very true for me, and perhaps I didn't care whether it was a novel or not.'

'Preston,' she said, 'you must try to understand me. I was not impatient because it was not a novel but because Wolfe did not see what it might have been – and if he really and truly had the passion you say he has, he would have seen because he would have really and truly felt it, and it would have taken its own form, and with his wonderful energy it would not have defeated him.'

162

A Conversation with Gertrude Stein

'What has passion got to do with choosing an art form?'

'Everything. There is nothing else that determines form. What Wolfe is writing is his autobiography, but he has chosen to tell it as a story and an autobiography is never a story because life does not take place in events. What he has really done is to release himself, and so he has only told the truth of his release and not the truth of discovery. And that is why he means so much to you young men, because it is your release too. And perhaps because it is so long and unselective it is better for you, for if it stays with you, you will give it your own form and, if you have any passion, that too, and then perhaps you will be able to make the discovery he did not make. But you will not read it again because you will not need it again. And if a book has been a very true book for you, you will always need it again.'

Her secretary came into the room, looked at her watch, and said: 'You have twenty-five minutes for your walk. You must be back at ten minutes to one.' I arose, suddenly conscious that, having asked for fifteen minutes out of her last day in America, I had stayed over an hour utterly unaware of time. I made to go.

'No,' she said abruptly, 'there is still more to say. Walk with me because I want to say it.' We went out of the hotel. 'Walk on my left,' she said, 'because my right ear is broken.' She walked very sturdily, almost rapidly, and shouted above the traffic.

'There are two particular things I want to tell you because I have thought about them in America. I have thought about them for many years, but particularly in America I have seen them in a new light. So much has happened since I left. Americans are really beginning to use their heads – more now than at any time since the Civil War. They used them then because they had to and thinking was in the air, and they have to use them now or be destroyed. When you write the Civil War you must think of it in terms of then and now and not the time between. Well, Americans have not gone far yet, perhaps, but they have started thinking again and there *are* heads here and something

163

is ahead. It has no real shape, but I feel it and I do not feel it so much abroad and that is why my business is here. You see, there is something for writers that there was not before. You are too close to it and you only vaguely sense it. That is why you let your economic problem bother you. If you see and feel you will know what your work is, and if you do it well the economic problem takes care of itself. Don't think so much about your wife and child being dependent upon your work. Try to think of your work being dependent upon your wife and child, for it will be if it really comes from you, and if it doesn't come from you – the *you* that has the wife and child and this Fifth Avenue and these people – then it is no use anyway and your economic problem will have nothing to do with writing because you will not be a writer at all. I find you young writers worrying about losing your integrity and it is well that you should, but a man who really loses his integrity does not know that it is gone, and nobody can wrest it from you if you really have it. An ideal is good only if it moves you forward and can make you produce, Preston, but it is no good if you prefer to produce nothing rather than write sometimes for money alone, because the ideal defeats itself when the economic problem you have been talking about defeats *you*.'

We were crossing streets and the crowds were looking curiously at this bronzed-faced woman whose picture had been so often in the papers, but she was unaware of them, it seemed to me, but extraordinarily aware of the movement around her and especially of taxicabs. After all, I reflected, she had lived in Paris.

'The thing for the serious writer to remember,' she said, 'is that he is writing seriously and is not a salesman. If the writer and the salesman are born in the same man it is lucky for both of them, but if they are not, one is sure to kill the other when you force them together. And there is one thing more.'

We turned off Madison Avenue and headed back to the hotel.

'A very important thing – and I know it because I have seen it kill so many writers – is not to make up your mind that you are any one thing. Look at your own case. You have written, first a biography, then a history of the American Revolution, and third a modern novel. But how absurd it would be if you should make up your mind that you are a Biographer, a Historian, or a Novelist!' She pronounced the words in tremendous capitals. 'The truth is probably that all those forms are dead because they have become forms, and you must have felt that or you would not have moved on from one to another. Well, you will go on and you will work in them, and sometime, if your work has any meaning and I am not sure that anything but a lifework has meaning, then you may discover a new form. Somebody has said that I myself am striving for a fourth dimension in literature. I am striving for nothing of the sort and I am not striving at all but only gradually growing and becoming steadily more aware of the ways things can be felt and known in words, and perhaps if I feel them and know them myself in the new ways it is enough, and if I know fully enough there will be a note of sureness and confidence that will make others know too.

'And when one has discovered and evolved a new form, it is not the form but the fact that *you are the form* that is important. That is why Boswell is the greatest biographer that ever lived, because he was no slavish Eckermann with the perfect faithfulness of notes – which are not faithful at all – but because he put into Johnson's mouth words that Johnson probably never uttered, and yet you know when you read it that that is what Johnson would have said under such and such a circumstance – and you know all that because Boswell discovered Johnson's real form which Johnson never knew. The great thing is not ever to think about form but let it come. Does that sound strange from me? They have accused me of thinking of nothing else. Do you see the real joke? It is the critics who have really thought about form always and I have thought about – writing!'

Gertrude Stein laughed enormously and went into the hotel with the crowd.

165

SAMUEL STEWARD

Samuel Steward was a student at Ohio State University when introduced to the works of Gertrude Stein by Clarence Andrews, his English professor, who spent six months of every year in his beloved France. Andrews himself had visited Stein and Toklas in Paris and returned to dazzle his students with anecdotes.

In 1932, Steward had the temerity of writing to Stein to inform her of Andrews's sudden death, generating a correspondence that evolved into a friendship. In 1937, after Steward had earned a doctorate in English literature and taught for several years in Montana and Washington, he made a long visit to Stein and Toklas in Bilignin.

In *Dear Sammy: Letters from Gertrude Stein and Alice B. Toklas,* Steward prefaces his collection of letters with a memoir recalling his tour of southern France with his two new friends, and his visits to Toklas after Stein's death. In the selection that follows, Steward and Stein are having a discussion about literature, especially Stein's. 'Everyone is fascinated with that little sign of yours – the tiny rose inside the circle of "rose is a rose is a rose," ' which Stein had engraved on her personal stationery. 'Why did you invent that?' Steward asked.

She laughed. 'I was wondering when you'd ask that. Most everyone who comes here on a visit asks it the first day.'

Jacques Lipchitz, *Gertrude Stein* (1920). Bronze, 17½
by 8¼ by 10 inches, including base. Collection, The
Museum of Modern Art, New York. Fund given by
friends of the artist. Photograph by Eric Pollitzer.

from *Dear Sammy*

'College experiments pure and simple, that's all they were. My teacher William James was interested in whether the unconscious mind could furnish messages, any sort of messages from what he called "the summer-land," and so Leon Solomons and I tried to test whether the un- or sub-conscious could produce writing under certain conditions of fatigue or reverie, or distraction. But I, I always knew what I was writing, it was not automatic.'

'And punctuation?' I asked.

'It's nonsense mostly. I already told you that everyone knows a question is a question so why use a question mark. And commas, they help you put on your coat and button your shoes for you and anyone can do that. But I believe in periods because after all you have to stop sometime.' She chuckled.

We had come to the bottom of the ravine and slowly started back up toward the old chateau.

'You really have two styles of writing,' I said.

'Maybe more than that,' Gertrude said. 'The style in the autobiographies is what I call my moneymaking style. But the other one is the main one, the really creative one.'

I ventured an analogy. 'It reminds me of the improvisations of Eastern music,' I said. 'It sort of goes on and on, maybe like water running,

From *Dear Sammy* by Samuel Steward (New York: Houghton Mifflin, 1977), 24–26. Reprinted by permission of Curtis Brown, Ltd. © 1977 by Samuel Steward.

a little different sometimes, mostly the same. And you wait for a cre-
scendo or a climax and none comes, and just when you begin to feel
thwarted, the music turns soothing and then there is a kind of twitch,
and it becomes really and truly interesting.'

'I like that Sammy, I really do,' Gertrude said. 'That is nice, you are
perspicace.'

We went on climbing. 'You know,' she said, 'you're going to Zurich
and I am going to give you a note to Thornton Wilder and you can
say hello to him. He's writing a play just now and I think it may be a
good one.'

'Thank you,' I said. 'I would like that.'

We reached the chateau, always more out of breath than when we
started, and had a very light evening meal. After it was over we sat
and rocked a while and talked in the living room, and then Gertrude
gave a mighty yawn.

'I'm sleepy that's what I am and tired too and I'm going to bed.'

FRANÇOISE GILOT

Françoise Gilot was twenty-one when, in 1943, she saw Pablo Picasso sitting with friends at a small restaurant in Paris. Gilot already was a painter, working then in a representational style that later gave way to more expressive forms. Although she felt immediately attracted to Picasso, she realized that his needs and desires would shape their future relationship. 'At the time I went to live with Pablo,' she recalled, 'I had felt that he was a person to whom I could, and should, devote myself entirely, but from whom I should expect to receive nothing beyond what he had given the world by means of his art. I consented to make my life with him on those terms.' But during their twelve years together, she came to reconsider her feelings of resignation.

By 1955, Gilot and Picasso had had two children, Claude and Paloma, but Picasso showed no signs of making a lasting commitment to his family. Indeed, Gilot heard rumors of liaisons with other women. Finally, when Gilot discovered that he had begun an affair with Jacqueline Roque – the woman with whom he spent the rest of his life – she left him.

Gilot was a vital part of the circle that surrounded Picasso, including artists, writers, and not a few sycophants. As she testifies in this excerpt from her memoir, *Life with Picasso,* she felt affection for Gertrude Stein, but, like many wives of Stein's famous male friends, suffered the disdain of Alice Toklas.

from *Life with Picasso*

That winter, Pablo had given me *The Autobiography of Alice B. Toklas* to read. I had found it very entertaining and told him I'd like to meet Gertrude Stein. One spring morning he said to me, 'We're going to see Gertrude this week. That will amuse you. Besides, I have a lot of confidence in her judgment. If she approves of you, that will reinforce whatever good opinion I might have of you.' From that moment on, I lost all desire to meet Gertrude Stein. But I had to go; he had made an appointment with her.

When the day arrived, I had lunch with Pablo at *Le Catalan*. He was unusually cheerful, but I couldn't swallow a thing. Toward 3:30 we climbed the broad, cold, exposed stairway of Gertrude Stein's house in the Rue Christine and Pablo knocked at the door. After a little wait, the door was opened a crack, almost grudgingly, like the door to the studio in the Rue des Grands-Augustins. Through the slit I saw a thin, swarthy face with large, heavy-lidded eyes, a long hooked nose, and a dark, furry mustache. When this apparition recognized Pablo, the door was opened wider and I saw a little old lady wearing an enormous hat. It was Alice B. Toklas.

She let us into the hallway and greeted Pablo in a deep baritone voice. When Pablo introduced me, she ground out a '*Bonjour, Made-*

From *Life with Picasso* by F. Gilot (New York: McGraw-Hill, 1964), 68–71.

moiselle,' with an accent that sounded like a music-hall caricature of an American tourist reading from a French phrase book. We took off our coats and hung them in a little vestibule. We passed into a larger gallery lined with paintings, many of them from the Cubist period and mostly by Pablo and Juan Gris. From that room we went into a salon flooded with sunlight. There, in an armchair facing the door, under her portrait painted by Pablo in 1906, sat Gertrude Stein, broad, solid, imposing, her gray hair cropped very close. She had on a long brown skirt to the ankles, a dull beige blouse, and her feet were bare inside heavy leather sandals.

Pablo presented me and she waved me to a seat on a horsehair divan facing her. Pablo sat on a window ledge beside and slightly behind her with his back to the light, as though he wanted to survey the scene yet not be obliged to participate. A gleam in his eyes indicated that he was expecting to enjoy himself immensely. Alice Toklas sat down on the divan beside me but as far away as possible. In the center of our little circle were several low tables covered with plates of *petits fours,* cakes, cookies, and all kinds of luxuries one didn't see at that period, right after the war.

I was intimidated by Gertrude Stein's first questions, which were a little sharp and sometimes obvious. It was quite clear that she was asking herself, What's going on between Pablo and this girl? And first in English and then in French – not very good French – she tried to get me to talk. It was worse than the oral examination for the *baccalauréat.*

I did my best with her questions but I was distracted by the enormous hat on Alice Toklas's head. She was dressed in very dark gray and black, and her huge hat was black with a little gray trim. She looked as though she had dressed for a funeral, but the tailoring was obviously of the very first quality. I learned afterwards that her couturier was Pierre Balmain. I felt ill at ease with her there beside me. She looked hostile, as though she were predisposed against me. She spoke infrequently, occasionally supplying Gertrude Stein with a detail. Her voice was very low, like a man's, and rasping, and one could hear the air passing loudly through her teeth. It made a most disagreeable sound, like the sharpening of a scythe.

As the afternoon went on, Gertrude Stein seemed more relaxed in her interrogation. She wanted to know how well I knew her work and whether I had read the American writers. Fortunately I had read quite a few. She told me she was the spiritual mother of them all: Sherwood Anderson, Hemingway, Scott Fitzgerald. She talked especially about Dos Passos as having been greatly influenced by her; even Erskine Caldwell. She wanted me to understand the importance of her influence, even on those who had never come to sit at her feet, like Faulkner and Steinbeck. She said that without her, there would be no modern American literature as we know it.

After straightening out the literary matters, she got around to the subject of painting and she began to cross-examine me on Cubism. With all the pedantry of my twenty-three years, I replied with whatever seemed the appropriate observations on analytic Cubism, synthetic Cubism, the influence of Negro art, of Cézanne, and so on. I wasn't trying to make a good impression on her; I simply wanted to make sure that Pablo didn't feel disappointed in me. Finally she turned and pointed to her portrait by Pablo and said, 'What do you think of my portrait?' I told her I knew her friends had thought that although in the beginning she didn't look like that, after a while she had come to resemble it. But after all those years, it seemed to me, she had begun to move in the other direction, I said, because she didn't resemble it any longer. Now she had come a lot closer to the idea I had of what a Tibetan monk ought to look like. She looked at me disapprovingly.

The most disturbing thing about the whole afternoon, though, was that while all this was going on, Alice Toklas was not sitting still, but bobbing up and down, moving back and forth, going out into the dining room to get more cakes, bringing them in, and passing them around. And she looked *so* glum at some of my answers to Gertrude

Stein. Perhaps they didn't seem respectful enough. I admired Gertrude Stein, but I could see no reason to play up to her. And so whenever I said anything displeasing to Alice Toklas, she would dart another plate of cakes at me and I would be forced to take one and bite into it. They were all very rich and gooey and with nothing to drink, talking was not easy. I suppose I should have said something about her cooking, but I just ate her cakes and went back to talking with Gertrude Stein, so I guess I made an enemy of Alice Toklas that day. But Gertrude Stein seemed, if I could judge from her hearty laughter, to find me rather entertaining, at least for the moment. At the end of the afternoon she left the room and came back with three of her books. One of them, I remember, was *Wars I Have Seen.* She wrote in them all, and in that one she wrote, 'Rose is a rose is a rose is a rose – once more for Françoise Gilot.'

When we got ready to leave, Gertrude Stein said to me, 'Now you can come to see me all by yourself.' And there was another dark look from Alice Toklas. I might have gone back if I hadn't been so terrorized by Miss Stein's little acolyte, but I was and so I promised myself never to set foot in that apartment again.

Throughout all this, Pablo had not said a word, although I could see his eyes sparkling and could read his thoughts from time to time. It was clear that he was just letting me skirt the quicksand to the best of my ability. When we got to the door on the way out, he said, quite innocently, 'Well, Gertrude, you haven't discovered any more painters lately?' She apparently sensed a trap, and said, 'What do you mean?' He said, 'Oh, no doubt about it, Gertrude, you're the grandmother of American literature, but are you sure that in the domain of painting you have had quite as good judgment for the generation that succeeded us? When there were Matisse and Picasso to be discovered, things went well. You finally got around to Gris, too, but since then, it seems to me your discoveries have been somewhat less interesting.'

She looked angry but made no answer. Just to stick the needle in a little deeper, Pablo said, 'You helped discover one generation and that's fine, but to discover two or three generations is really difficult and that I don't think you've done.'

There was a moment of silence and then she said, 'Look, Pablo, I tell a painter what is good in a painting of his and in that way I encourage him to keep on searching in the direction of his own special gift. As a result, what is bad disappears because he forgets it. I don't know if my critical judgment has lost its keenness or not, but I'm sure that my advice to painters has always been constructive.'

After that, I saw Gertrude Stein occasionally in the Rue de Buci, doing a bit of marketing around noontime. She seemed always to be wearing the same costume, covered by a cape, that I had seen her wear the day Pablo and I called on her. She always urged me, in a friendly way, to come see her in the Rue Christine. I would say, 'Oh, yes, yes,' but do nothing about it, because I found it easier to get along without her than to take her in tandem with Alice B. Toklas.

THERESE BONNEY

This rare eyewitness account of Gertrude Stein during World War II was published in *Vogue* in 1942. During the war, Stein was cut off from many of her friends and, because she and Toklas both were Jewish, in a precarious position during the French occupation by the Germans.

Stein's novel, *Mrs. Reynolds,* to which Bonney refers in this memoir, conveys to readers the sense of threat that both women faced. As Stein told Bonney, she portrayed Hitler and Stalin as characters in the novel, calling them Angel Harper and Joseph Lane, and exploring their sexual and psychological natures as well as their political actions. Difficult to read because of its flat tone and repetitions, *Mrs. Reynolds* nevertheless shows its heroine to be a courageous woman who survives the war – Stein does not identify the conflict as the Second World War – through a mixture of resignation and attention to work. 'There is nothing historical about this book except the state of mind,' Stein wrote in the book's epilogue.

Stein's reflections on war appear in other texts as well, including *Wars I Have Seen* and *Brewsie and Willie.*

Gertrude Stein
in France

I was looking for the masters of the École de Paris – for the great French artists of the pre-war world. Finding Gertrude Stein was a logical part of my quest. What had happened to her was as important as what had happened to them, and to me the answer had something very real to do with the fate of France.

I found her, months after the collapse of France, living in unoccupied territory, in a little village called Bilignin par Belley Ain, near Alsace. It is her ivory tower. She lives separated from her village, and her beloved France, only by an iron gate; the peasants, from far and wide, come to talk with her. And yet, she seems a person apart. And she is completely detached from the ephemeral politics of France today.

Detachment has never before been an important characteristic of Gertrude Stein. Constancy is her virtue. This is what is interesting about her: she has been faithful to a line of conduct, to a line of thinking, to an intuition – living fully, loyally, richly.

What she said in *Paris France,* her testament of love, might be brought to date and given as an explanation of why she stayed in France. She did not stay because she considered herself an expatriate, for she is not that in any sense of the word, or because she feared the impact of America. She stayed because she has found in Bilignin the

First published in *Vogue* (1 July 1942). Reprinted courtesy of Vogue. © 1942 (renewed 1970) by The Condé Nast Publications Inc.

'calm and peace that are necessary to her work.' I would add 'to her way of living.'

She sits in a great chair, seeming almost to preside over that 'way of living,' dressed in sombre, colourless, drab, ageless corduroys and tweeds, as she always has. Where she used to laugh prodigiously, infectiously, enormously – as all her friends know – today she smiles peacefully, humanly, sagely.

There are other changes, too. She is still surrounded by paintings, as she was in the early days at the rue de Fleurus in Paris, but her portrait by Picasso is now the most important painting, and the lovely nude young girl with flowers is no longer there. Practical problems bother her less. The bank in Baltimore is very far from Bilignin, but this preoccupation never seems to concern her deeply. Peasants in the village, strangers in the region, and even Picasso, who is renowned for his pinch-penny feeling about money, have all sent her messages. 'Credit for her,' one of them told me, 'until hell freezes over.'

Even when Bennett Cerf, her publisher, succeeds in sending her money – two hundred and forty-six, a hundred and ninety-three dollars – it goes to so many places in the world before it reaches her that it contributes little to the ever-recurring problem of balancing a budget. In one of her letters to America, she refers to the Odyssey of her dollars as 'an insoluble mystery.'

In January, 1941, she wrote to America, 'All the letters seem to get here . . . sometimes they get here quickly sometimes they come slowly but they all seem to get here which is very nice of them because it is very nice getting letters.' Again she writes, '. . . otherwise everything is serene just now.' When she wrote this, the Germans had been through her little village on their way south and again on their way north. France had fallen. 'We all live,' she continued, 'in hope there is plenty of that . . . we seem to quite like our country life, and we seem to have so many friends and new ones keep cropping up we have wood to burn and if we keep active we have enough to eat and luckily I like to walk . . . so life goes on day after day.'

When she writes 'keep active,' she means that she plants her potatoes, hoes them, weeds them, and digs them up. She digs the whole vegetable garden and kneads her own bread.

Many have asked me what Gertrude does for amusement, whether she is bored. She most certainly didn't seem bored. Her dogs, Pepe and Basket II., provide a certain amount of distraction for her and her companion, Alice Toklas. But friends are a great resource. 'In the fall,' she writes, 'Alice sits by the fire, and I saw wood; such is the daily occupation. We see lots of people to my great surprise.'

She reads hungrily – as she always did – detective and mystery stories. And of books, she writes to America, 'The books just came, and we were delighted to have them; you can get substitutes for most things, wood alcohol for essence, grape sugar for sugar, and other things for other things, but not anything for books . . . they did not take long to come either only a little more than a month.' And again, 'Have you *War and Peace* in the Modern Library, it would be interesting to read just now . . . I think I would like to read Gibbon's *Decline and Fall*.'

But Gertrude's greatest bulwark against boredom is, of course, her writing. She writes of her new book, 'You know I did start to write about how America looks to Europe I did a little bit, and then I began to put it in a novel I am doing now, and so I did not go on with it it might be fun to do, what do you think, well anyway the nightingales are singing and the frogs, and we are gardening and the potatoes are coming up, and we love you a lot, we do.' When I was there, she wrote to her publisher, 'I am going on with my new novel. I have twenty-five pages done, and Alice has begun typing, but it will be longish and of slow growth; it has both Hitler and Stalin in it.'

After I left, she had decided to call her novel *Mrs. Reynolds*. In another letter, she wrote, 'The heroine is something I called a publicity saint – the modern saint being somebody who achieves publicity without having done anything in particular, everybody told me I could not do it, without making her do something, but, by God I did, and I am proud.'

Outside the warm little world of writing and fireside, garden and iron gate, Gertrude plays a real part in the daily living of her countryside. The peasants told me that she goes to vintage with them, tastes the first fruits of the soil . . . the first pears, grapes.

Ford Maddox Ford wrote of Gertrude Stein in 1913, 'I saw Gertrude Stein driving with a snail-like precision her Ford car . . . the air of awfulness of a Pope or Pharaoh . . . Gertrude Stein was at that time the sun about which the plastic artists revolved more or less.' She still had a Ford when I last saw her, and she still drives at a snail's pace. Today again around her, and a handful of other Americans, the faith of the French people revolves – around those few who know them well enough not to doubt, to understand, and to stand by.

Since the day she said goodbye to the villagers, went to Lyon, arranged her passport so that she might leave, and then resolved to stay, she has, I believe, never regretted or doubted. She wrote that she had decided not to leave France because 'it would be awfully uncomfortable.'

That is all the reason she gives. But I think she stayed because she owed France a great gratitude and, like Matisse, Dufy, Bonnard, Maillol, and Lurçat, felt that she must stay with her friends there. Like everybody else in France today, she is very busy accommodating herself to everything, digging potatoes, writing – always convinced, as she wrote in 1940, that 'the Winner Loses.'

ERIC SEVAREID

Eric Sevareid first met Gertrude Stein in 1938, when he was living in Paris as a reporter, and later city editor, for the international edition of the *New York Herald Tribune.* Both Stein and Toklas were charmed by the twenty-six-year-old writer, and dismayed when they were cut off from him and many other young friends during World War II. In 1944, Sevareid, a war correspondent for CBS, was part of a group of about one hundred journalists who landed on the beaches between Toulon and Cannes with General Alexander Patch's U.S. Seventh Army.

On the morning of September 1, he asked his colleague Frank Gervasi, a reporter for *Collier's Weekly,* if he would like to join in the search for Gertrude Stein. Gervasi needed no convincing: besides wanting to see the legendary Stein, he also was eager to hear her opinion about Hemingway, whom he had just met in New York and did not like.

The search party included Sevareid, Gervasi, Price Day of the *Baltimore Sun,* and Newbold Noyes of the *Washington Star.* 'None of us could remember anything Stein had ever written except *The Autobiography of Alice B. Toklas,* and could quote only 'A rose is a rose is a rose,' and 'Pigeons on the grass alas,' Gervasi recalled. 'The four of us were fully aware of the fact, however, that we were on our way to meet an authentic genius, the inventor of "Steinese," who had influenced several important writers of our time.'

If they were excited about meeting Stein and Toklas, the two women, who had not been out of Culoz in two years, and who had lost touch with some of their closest friends, were equally excited about seeing the four Americans. Stein, Gervasi said, 'spread her arms in a welcoming embrace, and clamped them about me, nearly crushing my ribs, saying over and over again, "You don't know how glad I am to see you."' The group stayed for lunch, and when they left, Stein agreed to do a radio broadcast for Sevareid, and she gave Gervasi a newly typed manuscript of her latest piece, the witty and moving *Wars I Have Seen*. Although *Collier's* failed to publish it, Gervasi succeeded in routing it to his friend, the editor Bennett Cerf, who bought it for Random House.

from *Not So Wild a Dream*

It was the first of September, the anniversary of the war's beginning. I was thinking of Paris and those old days of peace, which already belonged to a previous era. For I was embarked on a search for Gertrude Stein, who had never left France and was believed to be hiding somewhere near the Alps. The first clue came in a telegram from Paul White in New York, who answered my inquiries by giving the address she was known to have had two years before. As it happened, the address was wrong by about twelve kilometers, and we would have had to search all day had it not been that the command car broke down as we headed toward the upper Rhone, an area we believed no Allied troops had entered. As we fussed helplessly with the engine, a jeep appeared from the direction of the river, to our great surprise. The jeep driver worked on our car, and the officer, Lieutenant Colonel Bill Perry, inspector general of the Forty-fifth, drew me aside. 'Good story down that way,' he said, and immediately I was afraid my little scoop was gone already. Perry had wandered into the area on an idle visit and as he stopped in the town of Belley, a woman laden with market bags came up to him and said: 'I'm Gertrude Stein. Who are you?' Perry had spent the night at her house, which was at Culoz, farther

Reprinted from *Not So Wild a Dream*, by Eric Sevareid (New York: Atheneum, 1976). Reprinted by permission of Don Congdon Associates, Inc. © 1946, renewed 1974 by Eric Sevareid.

north, and had just left her an hour before meeting us. He promised to give me a day before telling the story at headquarters.

The assistant mayor of Culoz directed us to the 'Dovecote,' Miss Stein's small château at the base of a towering, rocky hill. The same old brown velvet cap hung at the entrance way, but the poodle that answered the ring was not the same homely little mutt I remembered from Paris. Gertrude greeted us with a shout and a bearhug. The iron-gray hair was still closely cropped, and the small eyes were as direct and searching as before, but she was just a trifle more bent, a trifle heavier in her walk. Alice B. Toklas – 'Pussy' – was still soft, small, and warmly murmurous, but also a little more bowed. The big Picasso portrait of Gertrude dominated the spacious, sunlit living-room as it had previously dominated the small, dark parlor in Paris. The luncheon she served us was magnificent, the coffee decent, the sugar real. When we offered to give them army rations, Alice said: 'Keep it. Just give me one American cigarette and I will be happy.' We talked, of course, for hours and hours. Rather, Gertrude talked and we listened, and the process was as agreeable as ever before. She wished to fill in the great gap in the gossip that years of silence had interrupted, to know about Hemingway and Thornton Wilder and Woollcott and a dozen others. She did not know that Woollcott was dead, and when we said we had just seen Hemingway's wife, Alice sniffed and said: 'That makes his third wife. Tch, tch, tch.'

Germans had been living in Gertrude's house until recently, and it had been Italians the year before – 'but of course they don't count,' she said. When news came that Turin had been bombed, the Italian officer wept. 'Can you imagine it, his asking us for sympathy?' The Italians caught onto their American accents right away and said nothing, but the Germans were too stupid to realize they were dwelling with the enemy, and that the lady of the house was not only a Jewess but also a famous writer whose works were on Goebbels' blacklist. 'The German way,' said Gertrude, 'was to bang on the door and demand this room and this room and say "no answers, please" – not that anybody would ever try to answer them. They were just unpleasant at times but never really bad while they were here, only they had that terrible key complex. They were always going off with the keys, and then I would have to go to the locksmith again. It was such a bother.' One poor German soldier used to knock at the door and politely ask permission to walk in her garden.

She said that not everything about Vichy had been so bad. Many of the lower civil servants, like the mayor of Culoz, were perfectly wonderful. Gertrude had a faint tone of sorrow that Pétain had turned out so miserably, and she said it was when he let the Germans round up the young men for service in Germany that the people really turned against the old man. Laval was unspeakable, and for Darnand's vicious Gestapo not even Gertrude had adequate words. The mayor had always protected her secret from the Germans and so had all the people of the village, who knew perfectly well who and what she was. When the Germans began rounding up enemy aliens, the mayor simply forgot to tell them about the Stein household, because, he said to Gertrude, 'you are obviously too old for life in a concentration camp. You would not survive it, so why should I tell them?' He had long, handlebar mustaches and a small, bald head and was straight from comic opera. Yet he was a man of courage and decent feeling. When he came in to meet us it was hard for him to preserve his ramrod dignity and not weep in front of everyone.

As Gertrude described them, the occupying Germans were like a fog – something that was always there but which you walked right through and hardly saw or thought about. She confirmed what I had long suspected: that the Germans could never really understand the French, never really penetrate their subtle psychology, that they were in fact the very last Europeans capable of governing Europe. A German subaltern roomed for months with the French station master and was never aware that the man was chief of all the local *Maquis*. When a new German lieutenant took charge of the village he demanded of the mayor if there were *Maquis* on the mountain behind the village. The mayor assured him there were none, because there was no water on the mountain. 'When I go hunting there,' he said, 'I have to take a bottle of water for my dog.' The officer did not believe him, but after his men had spent several days searching the mountain, he said: 'You are right. There is no water on the mountain.' The mayor said to me: 'Of course, I did not tell him that men are not dogs and that men live on wine.'

For many months through the winter Gertrude was obliged to walk several miles a day for food, and there was a time when her funds ran perilously low, until a friend from Paris stopped by and bought Cézanne's portrait of his mother from Gertrude. With all the difficulties, the isolation from lifelong friends, these had been the happiest years of her life, she said, and one could only believe her. She felt she had come very close to the ordinary French people and had learned more about them in this sharing of their tribulations than in all her previous thirty years in the country. The village people had learned to share, not only their sorrows, but their little pleasures and their material goods in a way one would not have believed of the parsimonious French. If somebody's rooster disappeared, some villager, no matter how hungry his family might be, was certain to return it before very long. The worst time had come when the Germans began rounding up the boys of twenty, when every family was faced with a terrible decision. Most of the lads preferred to run away into the mountains, where they joined the *Maquis* if they did not die of hunger and exposure. The *Maquis'* secrets were wonderfully well kept, and even Gertrude, who knew every soul in the place, did not know until the dénouement – a pitched battle near her house in which fifty Germans were killed – which men were the *Maquis* leaders.

As she talked of these things, sometimes bursting into the old, gay laughter, sometimes almost in tears, a group of small children banged on her door. They wanted permission to play '*Maquis*' in her grounds. The game consisted in pointing a wooden gun and saying: 'Bop, bop, bop – ça y est!'

She told us how so many of the fathers, veterans of the last war, were sick at heart when their youngsters wished to go underground, risking the firing squads. 'But,' she said, 'the children tried to explain to their parents that the old ones did not understand this war, that this was the young ones' war, and that the firing squad meant absolutely nothing to them. Anyway,' Gertrude went on, 'this war makes a whole lot more sense than the last one, which was very dull. This is a logical war and it is a far more interesting one.'

She was just then finishing a new book, begun after France was defeated and her exile commenced. It was a book about all the wars she had known, from reading and in life, and its theme, as far as we could gather, was that wars come because every century tries to destroy itself. Hitler, she said, was essentially a nineteenth-century person, and his war had destroyed the nineteenth century. She had scribbled the book in large, bound ledgers, and since her sprawling handwriting baffles everyone but Alice B. Toklas, she had little fear that the Germans would discover it. When Paris was liberated, Alice began copying on the typewriter 'like mad.' Gertrude had always said she would end the book with the appearance of the first Americans at her house – 'I always knew they would come, I always knew that war correspondents would be here, I never doubted it for one single moment' – and she had kept her promise. She gave the manuscript to Frank Gervasi of *Collier's,* who was with me.

I interrupted her flow of talk about Hitler to remind her of our prewar conversation in which she had asserted that Hitler was not dangerous because he was only a German romanticist, who wanted the feelings of triumph but would never go through the blood bath to get it. Miss Stein hesitated only a moment, then went on with the thread of her conversation, pretending not to have heard me.

187

When she said goodbye to us in the command car and we had turned away, Private Bill, our hardheaded driver from Boston, said: 'Who 'n hell is that old battle-ax?' We said it was Gertrude Stein, and he replied: 'That beats the – out of me,' which is G.I. for 'That's beyond me.'

We came to fetch her two days later, to take her the forty miles to Voiron so that she could broadcast for me to the United States. This was the farthest she and Alice B. had been from Culoz for at least two years, and the eyes of these two elderly women shone like the eyes of children on a picnic. She was, of course, something of a sensation in the press camp, dampened when the other reporters discovered that we had sent our dispatches about her forty-eight hours before. Her radio speech, in part, went like this:

What a day is today that is what a day it was day before yesterday, what a day! I can tell everybody that none of you know what this native land business is until you have been cut off from that same native land completely for years. This native land business gets you all right. Day before yesterday was a wonderful day. First we saw three Americans in a military car and we said are you Americans and they said yes and we choked and we talked, and they took us driving in their car, those long awaited Americans, how long we have waited for them and there they were Lieu- tenant Olsen and Privates Landry and Hartze and then we saw another car of them and these two came home with us, I had said can't you come home with us we have to have some Ameri- cans in our house and they said they guessed the war could get along without them for a few hours and they were Colonel Perry and Private Schmalz and we talked and patted each other in that pleasant American way and everybody in the village cried out the Americans have come the Americans have come and indeed the Americans have come, they have come, they are here God bless them. Of course I asked each one of them what place they came from and the words New Hampshire and Chicago and Detroit and Denver and Delta Colorado were music in our ears. And then four newspaper men turned up, naturally you don't count newspaper men but how they and we talked we and they and they asked me to come to Voiron with them to broadcast and here I am.

. . . You know I thought I really knew France through and through but I did not realize what it could do what it did in these glorious days. Yes I knew France in the last war in the days of their victories but in this war in the days of defeat they were much greater. I can never be thankful enough that I stayed with them all these dark days, when we had to walk miles to get a little extra butter a little extra flour when everybody somehow managed to feed themselves, when the *Maquis* under the eyes of the Germans received transported and hid the arms dropped to them by parachutes, we always wanted some of the parachute cloth as a souvenir, one girl in the village made herself a blouse of it.

It was a wonderful time it was long and it was heartbreaking but every day made it longer and shorter and now thanks to the land of my birth and the land of my adoption we are free, long live France, long live America, long live the United Nations and above all long live liberty, I can tell you that liberty is the most important thing in the world more important than food and clothes more important than anything on this mortal earth, I who spent four years with the French under the German yoke tell you so.

I am so happy to be talking to America today so happy.

SELECTED WORKS BY GERTRUDE STEIN

"Before the Flowers of Friendship
Faded Friendship Faded"
"Cultivated Motor Automatism"
"Eating"
"The Gertrude Stein Birthday Book"
"The Gradual Making of the Making
of Americans"
"If You Had Three Husbands"
"In the Red Deeps"
"A Little Called Pauline"
"Normal Motor Automatism"
"One"
"Pink Melon Joy"
"A Seltzer Bottle"
"Suppose an Eyes"
"A Village Are You Ready Yet
Not Yet"
"What Are Masterpieces and Why
Are There So Few of Them"

As Fine As Melanctha
The Autobiography of Alice B. Toklas
*A Book Concluding with 'As a Wife
Has a Cow A Love Story'*
Brewsie and Willie
Everybody's Autobiography
Four Saints in Three Acts
The Geographical History of America
Geography and Plays
How Writing Is Written
Lectures in America
A Long Gay Book
Lucy Church Amiably
The Making of Americans
Mrs. Reynolds
Painted Lace
Paris, France
Picasso
*Portrait of Mabel Dodge at the
Villa Curonia*
Reflection on the Atomic Bomb
Tender Buttons
Things As They Are
Three Lives
Wars I Have Seen

INDEX

Index